PRAISE FOR THE ORIGINAL *MENTAL MUSCLE*

"Why does *Mental Muscle* have such appeal? I think the reason is structure, simplicity, and accountability. Since each week's directive builds upon the previous week's work, we participants don't actively realize how deep the work is going, and how much change we are experiencing. At the completion of these sixteen weeks of consistent spiritual practice, when invited to review the breadth of work done the mental shifts are clear: Life has gotten better. ... Doing the work, guarantees living the results." - Rev. Dr. Jonathan Zenz

"James Mellon's Spiritual Boot Camp is exactly what the name implies, a focused, regular, structured set of guidelines for getting in shape – MENTAL shape. It's not the map for your life's journey, that's your choice, but it is the halogen headlights that light up the direction you're heading, which allows you to see clearly to your best choices. It takes intention, dedication, and heart, and it's worth every moment." - Mark Wyrick

"*Mental Muscle* has really forced me to show up for myself. And only by doing that have I been truly able to show up for anybody else." - Jeff Elam

"*Mental Muscle* has personally transformed my life." - Dr. Joe Hooper

"The journey is enlightening, revealing, liberating, and inspiring. It's one of the best things I've ever done for myself." - Janet Fontaine

"*Mental Muscle* pushed me into the recesses of my mind where I had buried my truth, my passion and my purpose." - Stephanie Lodge

"In committing myself to *Mental Muscle*, I now actually do the things I say I'm going to do. I deserve the best." - Laurie Gelman

"James Mellon's *Mental Muscle* was a revelation to me. I developed great insight into myself and learned to home in on what was truly important in this life. I strongly recommend this course for anyone seeking spiritual renewal and the freedom to create the life you want. It really is a decision to move forward." - Andre Barron

"*Mental Muscle* encouraged me every day to dig into the grass roots of my beliefs. It taught me to question, to reflect, to meditate, to listen, to hear, to observe, to commit, to intend, to be patient. More love flowed from me for others than I have ever felt – and most of all – an unfamiliar feeling swept over me – I felt love for myself." - Cherry Davis

"Boot Camp taught me a new way to look at my life, and how I choose to live it. It also gave me the tools to break free of my addiction. I have truly begun to live the life I had imagined." - Al Cook

"My mental muscle is now far stronger than my physical muscle. What an amazing journey to the center of me!" - Suzanne Benoit

"*Mental Muscle* made me realize that it's always about me. I was always looking outside of myself for someone else to create my experience. Not anymore!" - Randy Fuhrman

"I found *Mental Muscle* to be enormously beneficial. I became aware of habitual patterns of thought and behavior. The commitment to awareness over 16 weeks changed sporadic attempts at growth into lasting change." - Bob Morrisey

15TH ANNIVERSARY EDITION

MENTAL MUSCLE

16 Weeks of Spiritual Boot Camp

DR. JAMES MELLON

Print ISBN: 979-8-9868407-0-3
ebook ISBN: 979-8-9868407-1-0

092722

For My Family

Kevin, William & Nora

YOUR JOURNEY

ASK YOURSELF

What if I knew I was successful ...

... and that's all I knew?

What if I knew I was rich ...

... and that's all I knew?

What if I knew I was insanely talented ...

... and that's all I knew?

What if I knew my body was vibrant with perfect health ...

... and that's all I knew?

What if I knew I deserved to be happy ...

... and that's all I knew?

THAT is what you are here to KNOW!

FOREWORD

Ralph Waldon Emerson wrote, *"The mind, once stretched by a new idea never returns to its original dimensions."* The book you are holding, *Mental Muscle: 16 Weeks of Spiritual Boot Camp* is that new idea. It will stretch your mind, and I guarantee it will never return to its original dimensions. Instead, this book will change your life forever. It will put you in charge of your destiny.

I know this to be true because I experienced Mental Muscle firsthand on the very first day it was offered in 2007. I have worked the program over and over ever since, actively and enthusiastically applying its lessons to my own life. Each time I worked it, I went deeper, peeling away the layers of limitation that held me back. I became a conscious thinker in charge of my destiny.

I was a very different person then than I am today. I didn't know my beliefs were holding back my progress in life. Through Mental Muscle, I discovered those limiting beliefs and eliminated them once and for all. The creation and empowerment of my new belief system is what led me to the life of my wildest dreams here on the island of Kaua`i.

If you are brave and willing to delve deeply into yourself, this book holds the answers you seek. Applying each of its weekly principles will surface the illusionary walls that might be standing in the way of the life of *your* wildest dreams. All that is hindering your progress will be replaced with the Truth of your life – abundance, health, creativity and love (with generous sprinkles of adventure, exhilaration and contentment).

Dr. James conceived of this book with one intention: to focus our attention on the greatness that already is within us and to wipe away everything else that stands in its way.

Dr. James is able to do this because he practices and works his own mental muscle. I have witnessed his life both as a friend and a student, and now as a colleague. I know he stood the test of challenges that broke him into a million pieces – and still declares with certainty, "My faith in Principle stands unbroken." His life exemplifies the Truth that only through conscious thinking can we rise above the relative world to a higher order of being.

You will find his tried-and-tested truth in this book, a Universal Truth that, as Ernest Holmes put it, *"Our beliefs set the limit of our demonstration of a principle which, of Itself, is without limit."*

If you apply this Truth to your own life, you will have the same opportunity – the gift of unlimited and everlasting peace and wholeness as your constant companion, *no matter what* goes on in the outside world.

Don't be afraid to work your mental muscle. By flexing it, you tap into the Power of Source Energy that lies within you – your very Soul. And by flexing it *daily* for 16 weeks, you *awaken* and *energize* that Power within you.

Thank you Dr. James for giving me the lifetime tools I continue using every day. Life just gets better and better!

Love and Aloha,
Rev. Rita Andriello-Feren
Co-Spiritual Director, Center for Spiritual Living Kaua'i
Spiritual Coach
New Thought Author

INTRODUCTION

This whole journey began on one bright Sunday morning as I was driving to deliver that week's message to my spiritual community in North Hollywood, California.

I was stopped at a red light, and I looked across the road to a park where people were working out. Some ripped trainer guy was yelling at a group of people to DROP TO THE GROUND, JUMP BACK UP, RUN IT OUT, KNEES TO YOUR CHEST, ON YOUR BACK, SIT UPS!!! I was breaking a sweat just listening to him. "Wow," I thought, "what if I had some guy in my mind who constantly kept me on track, wouldn't let me slack off, made me stop complaining, never took 'no' for an answer, always held me to what I SAID I WANTED TO DO? What would THAT be like?" I mean, think about it, if I spent as much time on my Spiritual Practice as I do on my body, things would really change. My mind started to crackle with ideas.

What if I created a Boot Camp for the mind? What if I policed my mental capacity for creativity on a daily basis? What if I built strength and resistance to be able to lift myself above any perceived obstacle? What if I spent as much time on my INNER life as I do on my OUTER life? What if?

WHAT IF?

From those two words came the idea of *Mental Muscle -16 Weeks of Spiritual Boot Camp.* I knew that I had to create this thing. I had no idea what it would be, other than POWERFUL. And that was enough.

I announced it in church that morning. As the Founding Pastor of a New Thought church in Los Angeles, I knew there would be others who felt as I did. I asked for 10 people to take this journey with me. A journey of Truth! This was not for the faint of heart. I would require commitment – commitment to the Self. This wasn't going to be something you could try and see if you liked it or not. If you didn't like it, TOUGH! You signed up, now you have to finish it. After all, it is BOOT CAMP!

I was pretty amazed when the first Boot Camp was filled within minutes of my announcement. In fact, there was a waiting list. Clearly, this was an idea whose time had come. Now it was time for me to get in there and figure it out. The following pages illustrate what has come from the past 15 years of Spiritual Boot Camp. I am sure there is more to know, more to be, more to explore and more to sweat out. But I'll tell you one thing I **ABSOLUTELY KNOW,** if you follow this 16-week Boot Camp, you will never be the same again. Your **Mental Muscle** will be flexed and ready to carry whatever weight this world throws your way.

The following pages will guide you through Spiritual Boot Camp. It is a 16-week transformative experience that will pump you up, turn you inside out and strengthen you in such a way that Life will become what it was always meant to be: AWESOME!

They say that knowledge is power. What they say is correct. But unless you are ready to take that knowledge and put it to use, what good is it, really?

If you're ready to take your life in a new direction, if you're ready to take control of your mind and create a tomorrow that **YOU DESIGN**, if you're ready to put some MENTAL SWEAT into your Spiritual/Mental creative muscle, then this is for you.

Make the commitment! Take the challenge! Strengthen your Mental Muscle! **TURN TO THE NEXT PAGE**, literally!

WHAT IS SPIRITUAL BOOT CAMP

A journey to the Truth. Not anyone else's truth, but your Truth. There is something inside of you that drives you forward, pushes you to reach out and stretch your imagination. Every desire you've ever had, every dream you've ever contemplated, and every future you've ever stepped into, was backed by a Force within your mind. It all begins with YOU. The question is, do you recognize yourself within your own life?

In Spiritual Boot Camp, you are asked to go fearlessly into the mind and seek out the origins of your individual personality. Why do I react this way? Why do I always do this or that? What is my intention? Do I believe in what I say? Can I make a decision and stick to it? What are my beliefs? How are those beliefs running my life? Can I? Will I? Dare I?

YES! You can! You will! And Dare Away!

> *"What mind can conceive, man can achieve!"*
> *Ralph Waldo Emerson*

What can you conceive for your life right here in this moment? Who do you know yourself to be? What are you willing to achieve? Mental Muscle is designed to bring you face to face with yourself. It's an opportunity to eliminate years of accumulated B.S. and uncover an authentic Self that was, is and always will be right where you are. You just have to be willing to look in the mirror and be honest with what you see.

Mental Muscle is a regimen of honest, rigorous self-study, self-realization. Everything you need is right where you are. It's not 'out there.' It's something you discover within. You just have to be daring enough to go there.

Once you get an idea of who you are, and how you operate in the world, you can start deciding who you want to be and how you want to live.

It's YOUR CHOICE, not anyone else's. That's the first thing to realize.

YOU ARE AT CHOICE! YOU DECIDE!

But first, you have to be willing to GET DIRTY!

In the very first Mental Muscle, about halfway through the first 16-week journey, one of the group shared that he felt "as if all of my life I've been walking around in a white suit that I was afraid to get dirty." So I said, "It's time we all got dirty! Enough of the Sunday clothes. We need clothes we can muddy up." We needed to be fearless. We needed clothes we could muddy up. We needed bodies that weren't afraid to fall down, skin our knees and come up laughing. We needed to LIVE LIFE TO THE FULLEST. FEARLESS! EXPECTANT! JOYOUS!

> *"Our greatest glory is not in never failing,*
> *but in rising every time we fall."*
> *Confucius*

In other words, we needed to **NOT** be afraid to fall down. After all, sometimes it's the hardest fall that gives us the deepest perspective. So, are you ready to GET DIRTY?

LET'S DO IT!

PRE-TRAINING

The Life Force in you is bursting at the seams, waiting for you to open the floodgates, and let IT out. But, before we get started, there are three directives that you must begin to work. They are as follows:

RELEASE • LET GO • ALLOW

RELEASE all preconceived ideas you have of yourself. I don't care if you have never succeeded at anything in your entire life, it doesn't matter. Release what you think you know, and start every day with the mantra:

I know nothing. Now what can I learn?

You are then starting from a position of power.

LET GO of the past. Good, bad, or indifferent, the past is something that has no power other than the power YOU give it. Nothing can stop you quicker than if you spend your time looking back. You have arrived at this moment in time, and whatever got you here is not as important as what will get you there (wherever you decide "there" is). And believe it or not, your past doesn't dictate your future. Not unless you let it. The only thing that matters in this moment is the PRESENT. So, give yourself a present and let go of the past.

ALLOW something within you, the very thing that got you here, that nudged you to go deeper, allow "that" to take over. Allow yourself to know yourself, maybe for the first time. Allow yourself to remember who you are, who you've always been and who you've been waiting to become. Let that version of "You" step into the driver's seat for the next 16 weeks.

RELEASE • LET GO • ALLOW

It truly doesn't matter what your Spiritual Practice is. This is not about religion. It's about YOU. It's about the place you hold in whatever understanding you have of the Universe and this thing called Life. Regardless of what has come before, you are at the threshold of what will follow from this moment on. By using the tools demonstrated during the next 16 weeks, you will choreograph the most exquisite dance of Life you could ever imagine. And if you don't dance, just jump around a bit. If I've learned anything from Boot Camp, it's that I cannot and will not define myself as someone who does or doesn't do anything. I am limitless potential!

Life is waiting for YOU to HAPPEN! Don't wait for IT! It's already here.

Get dirty! Get to know yourself.

After all: If not now, **WHEN?**

THE MENTAL MUSCLE PROGRAM

It's simple, really. You show up in your own life, do the work necessary to know the Truth about who you are, and make changes based on what you now know. The first step is to SHOW UP. Our motto at Mental Muscle is:

DO THE WORK – LIVE THE RESULTS!

The problem is that many people want results without having to do the work. Let me be very clear, if you don't do the work, you don't reap the results. It's that simple!

So, what is the work? The program is a twice-weekly, one-hour session (one-on-one with the book, or with a group of people doing Boot Camp together). Each week, you will follow a specific regimen designated to create a firm, rooted Spiritual/Mental practice. You will examine your beliefs, your habits, your excuses; all the "stuff" that currently creates your life experience. It is very important that you do not get hung up on doing it "right." Just do it! Let something in you that knows, guide you. Make the changes you need to make in your life, swiftly, fearlessly and with a sense of humor. Yes, you need to be able to hold what's going on LIGHTLY.

Note: *If you are facilitating a Mental Muscle Boot Camp: Your only job is to listen and *allow* the session to play itself out. Be very careful "not" to turn it into a group therapy session. This is not therapy, it is an excursion into the recesses of the subconscious mind, mining for core beliefs that are somehow still running the show. Your overall objective is to find the core beliefs that no longer serve and replace them with ones that **DO**!

"The life which is unexamined is not worth living."
Plato

Repeat to yourself: **TODAY, I DECIDE TO LIVE FULLY!**

Today is about the decision to take your life into your own hands. No longer are you interested in living worn out dreams or expectations that, perhaps, aren't even yours. Success, prosperity, love, creativity, self-expression – Mental Muscle is an open door to wherever you decide to go. No one other than YOU will make the difference. And that is **GOOD NEWS!**

The Five Building Blocks

Meditation
Communication
Intention
Attention
Accountability

These first directives will be the foundation for all you will achieve in these next 16 weeks. They are your sacred tools. They are your drills, hammers and chisels that will excavate all of what makes you who you are and produce all that you know you can be. They are the way to Freedom.

Here's how it works:

On Day One of each week, you will be given an *Intention.* Following the *Intention*, you will be given a list of specific directives to follow throughout the week. You will check in a few days later, mid-week, to focus on your progress. This is what we call Day Two.

Make sure you schedule two or three days between your sessions to enable you to accomplish the work. On Day One of the following week, you will conclude the work of the previous week, as well as receive your *Intention* for the upcoming week.

Whether you do it alone or with a group of fellow Boot Campers, it is imperative that you stick to our schedule for the entire 16-week course. Remember, this is a commitment to yourself, and you owe it to YOU to succeed, no one else.

Meditation

At the start of each session, begin with 10 minutes of *Meditation*. And before you start squirming at the thought of sitting in a lotus position, all "pretzeled up" and uncomfortable, let me say that meditation is a personal thing. The purpose of it is to calm your mind, to quiet the voices, to hear the only voice worth hearing, your higher Self.

So, whatever it takes to accomplish that directive, that will be your meditation. It might be soothing music, candlelight, or a quiet atmosphere. It could be a walk in the park, a hike on a mountain path, swimming, walking the dog or merely staring out at the ocean. One woman liked to do jigsaw puzzles while another would play a djembe (drum). Once, one of our Boot Campers got so relaxed sitting in a chair listening to music that he fell off the chair and landed on the floor – luckily, it was carpeted.

In whatever way it works for you, your job is to accomplish the directive. Find a way to quiet the world around you and prepare for the rest of the hour. You will be provided with a quote that you can choose to take into your meditation.

Give yourself permission to drop into the most beautifully warm and soothing pool of consciousness. Just drop into a state of quiet, peaceful, gentle breathing and stay focused on nothing but your breath.

Communication

Each day you're asked to communicate with yourself in the form of a journal. This isn't a diary or a to-do list. It's a tell-it-like-it-is flow of consciousness designed to bring your B.S. into focus and show you what's up. I recommend that you do this first thing in the morning before you have time to think, either before or immediately after you meditate. Just let your mind empty out onto the page, that might be filled with the night's images or the day's priorities. It might be as simple as, "I hate writing." Regardless of what you write, it is important that you write. Journaling is a vibrant part of our Boot Camp and helps extract thoughts – beliefs – that are caught in the subconscious layer of our overall consciousness. This seems to be one of the hardest things for people to commit to during the process. And yet, it is incredibly important to keep track of your progress as you shift from one belief to another. Trust me, when you get to the final day of Boot Camp, you will be so glad you have an accounting of the journey. Whether you write in the morning or not, find the time to do the work each day. It doesn't have to be a novel, just your own personal thoughts. And keep it real. Don't write about flowers if that's not your experience. If you're in hell, write about the flames.

Side note: I have created a companion journal page for *Mental Muscle*. You can download this page at jamesmellon.org/bookresources.

If you are doing this in a group, each member of the group takes an agreed-upon amount of time to communicate what is going on with them. Keep it to a minimum and don't allow yourself to go off on tangents that don't concern the directive. Remember, we are about the business of directing our thoughts to a constructive place of transformation. That doesn't mean filtering your life through rose-colored glasses. Tell the facts as they are – but leave the drama behind.

There is **ABSOLUTELY NO CROSSTALK!**

To be clear and so there is no confusion: Crosstalk is the way we usually communicate in modern-day society. Unfortunately, that doesn't make it right or healthy. We've made it acceptable to butt into one another's points of view. We interject in the middle of someone else's sentences, expressing our agreement or objection before there's anything to agree or object to. This causes the person speaking to veer off their point, lose their place or even retreat out of a sense of fear or doubt. It stops the natural flow of the thought process.

During Mental Muscle, respect one another and allow for the authentic voice to have its say unencumbered by outside interference.

And if you're doing this alone, don't interrupt yourself. Give yourself the freedom to write, say, think whatever wants to come up. You just might surprise yourself with what's in there.

Intention

Next is the weekly *Intention*. This is the global directive for the week. Each week, you will have a specific intention on which to focus. These intentions are designed to reveal your personal belief system. As you stay conscious of your intention, you will watch as it plays itself out in your everyday affairs. You will be amazed at how much is going through your mind on a day-by-day basis. Your beliefs are directing your thoughts, which are creating your experience, even as you sit reading this sentence. Each *Intention* is designed to bring you more clarity on what you're doing with your mind. Now THAT is exciting news. That's something to look at!

Attention

This brings us to the next directive: *Attention*. In the world of Quantum Mechanics, we are introduced to the concept that what we focus on expands. What we put our attention on, then, grows. If you continually put your attention on how much you don't have, you continue to find situations where you don't have. If, conversely, you put your attention on what you **DO** have, you are stimulating the energy field of prosperity and you manifest more. I know I'm simplifying this greatly, but in truth, it is that simple. What you focus on expands, **NO MATTER WHAT!**

What you put your **ATTENTION** on is a vital part of the work we do in Mental Muscle. In fact, once you start really paying attention to what you pay attention to, you'll be surprised at what those things are. You'll also be able to see why your life is the way it is. **AND,** most importantly, you'll be able to start putting your **ATTENTION** where you want it to be, on your highest and greatest good. In that way we begin to master the Law of Cause and Effect, which says that ...

Accountability

Once you start on the road to freedom, building your mental muscle, enriching, and strengthening your Spiritual life, it is imperative that you follow the most important directive of Boot Camp: **Accountability.** From the Latin *accomptare* (to account), accountability is your promise to yourself to account for your actions, decisions, and results. Dan Zedra, author of the best-selling book "Think Big,"writes this about accountability:

> *"Some favorite expressions of small children:*
> *It's not my fault ... They made me do it ... I forgot.*
> *Some favorite expressions of adults:*
> *It's not my job ... No one told me ... It couldn't be helped ...*
> *True freedom begins and ends with personal accountability."*

I thought this quote was appropriate, given some of the excuses I have heard in Boot Camp over the past 15 years. The most common obstacle to self-awareness, and subsequently to personal responsibility, is the notion that something is out of your control. This is not true. While it is true that you cannot change another person or rewrite history, you are always in the power seat in your own life. You have the power to **react** in whatever way you decide to react. You may not be able to change what has happened, but you can certainly change **how** you react to the situation. That is personal Power.

Mental Muscle is here to help you recover this essential and life-altering Power!

**TODAY, I DECIDE TO LIVE FULLY!
I BEGIN NOW!**

I would like to suggest that you do not read the rest of this book in advance of doing the work. Each week is designed to focus your mind on a given Intention. We are seeking clarity, understanding and intuition. There is plenty of noise in this world to pollute the mind and keep it so distracted that it doesn't have the capacity to consciously create. Oh, we're creating, alright. We're *always* creating. But deliberate, conscious thinking is far more powerful than reactive thinking.

Take each week as it comes and work it like you've never worked anything before. Keep your mind focused on the Intention at hand and the tasks you will be given. ***Allow*** yourself to experience the journey, every moment of the way. See yourself at the end of this 16-week Bootcamp replenished, revitalized, reborn. ***Release*** the past and create the future. It all begins in this present moment. ***Let Go*** of anything that could hold you back. There is nowhere to go but forward. Forward with ***Confidence!***

> *"If one advances confidently in the direction of his dreams,
> and endeavors to live the life which he has imagined,
> he will meet with a success unexpected in common hours."*
> *Henry David Thoreau*

WEEK ONE
YOUR WORD

WEEK ONE

DAY ONE

Meditation: 10-minute minimum

Take the following quote with you into your meditation. Allow your mind to release all unwanted thoughts and consider these words.

> *"I like to think of enlightenment as a never-ending horizon.*
> *You get close to it and then another horizon shows up."*
> *Deepak Chopra*

Communication: What thoughts came up during your meditation? Were you able to relax and let go? How in control of your own mind are you? As you begin Spiritual Boot Camp, allow yourself to stay completely open to what flows through your mind.

- Write your thoughts, without judgment, in your journal. You do not need to be brilliant, only honest. There is no wrong way to do this – other than not to do it. Empty your mind and see what's going on in there. Put it down in words for reference later.

- If you are in a group, share your thoughts (keeping mindful of your time allotment). No cross-talking. Opinions are useless. We are about the business of revealing Truth, which is personal to each of us.

- Write down what you want from this Boot Camp experience. Why are you taking this journey?

Intention: This week's Intention is **Your Word.**

Today you will choose a word that will become your intention for the entire 16-week Boot Camp. Everyone has a **Word** within them. Something that is pressing against their conscious mind with such force and passion that it almost aches to be released. It can be quite subtle in its desire to be known, or it can be a brass band marching through the parade that is your mind. Either way, it's there.

Your **Word** can be an inner longing, a forgotten dream, a deep desire. It is the reason you're taking this Boot Camp. It is what you want most. You might not even be conscious of what it is in this present moment. Not a problem. There is something within you that knows.

- If you are doing this on your own, take a moment here and "listen" to your thoughts. Ask yourself:

What do I want?

Write it down. Add this to your journal. Let yourself be free from any conditions or past experiences. You get to claim what you want. Go for it without any limitations whatsoever.

- Group work: Each person gets a moment to reflect on their reason for taking this Boot Camp.

What came up? Did a specific **Word** emerge? Within your wants and desires, is there an idea whose time has come? Perhaps it's an emotion or a feeling that you wish to pursue. Chances are you have already thought of Your **Word**. Very often, they have a way of choosing us. This happens when Intuition steps in and aligns us with our highest good. Frequently in Boot Camp, Your **Word** comes as soon as I suggest it. And sometimes it takes a while. Again, don't worry about it. You might have to listen a bit to find the **Word** that fits. Not a problem. Your **Word** is already there. Just **allow** it to come forward.

Some **Words** revealed in Boot Camp:

Commitment
Release
Believe
Authentic
Flow
Soar
Peace
Detachment
Purification
Felicity
Focus
Expand
Blastoff
Discover
Impeccability
Love
Maya

Each of these **Words** represents a personal journey – a commitment to knowing more, revealing more, understanding more. Whatever **Your Word** may be, it is backed by a determination to explore its meaning in your life. There is nothing more important than your life. Starting today, there is nothing more important than **Your Word**.

Other than to fellow Boot Campers, I suggest that you keep **Your Word** to yourself. No one's opinion matters but your own. So **allow** your thoughts to be just that, your thoughts.

Attention/Accountability: How we pay **attention** to our **intentions** determines how and if they will materialize in our lives. Making the decision to do something, without the act of actually "doing it" is what keeps most people sitting in front of their television sets living other people's lives. The following is a list of directives that will give you the opportunity to "activate" your **intention**.

Directives for the Week:

1. Each morning, when you wake up, before you do anything or say anything to anyone, write your initial thoughts in your journal. Again, they don't have to be brilliant, they just have to be honest. This is nothing more than a mental dump, to free space for you to design your day.

2. Work with **Your Word** throughout the week. Make a conscious decision to remember **Your Word** at least three times throughout each day.

3. Before going to bed, in that moment right before you close your eyes and drift into dreamland, remind yourself of **Your Word**.

Remember: What you tell yourself is far more important than what others tell you.

Keep Your Word!

WEEK ONE

DAY TWO

Meditation: Bring **Your Word** into your meditation. Allow its energy to focus your mind. If you find yourself wandering, gently bring yourself back by once again focusing on **Your Word**.

> *"Self-trust is the first secret of success."*
> *Ralph Waldo Emerson*

Begin to trust your inner "knower." There is something within you, call it Intuition, that is readily available at all times. Put it to work for you! **Allow** it to inform you of your highest good.

Communication: What has come up since you found **Your Word**? Does it feel like the right word? Have you had an urge to change it? Are you having trouble owning it? Do you believe (I mean, really believe) that it is attainable, whatever it is? How has it begun to play out in your everyday life?

- Write down your answers to these questions and whatever else is going through your mind regarding **Your Word**.

Intention: It's always amazing to me when someone in the group chooses a word, and just the choice alone causes an atomic reaction to take place in their life. In one Boot Camp I chose the word "detachment." I can't tell you how many things I suddenly realized I needed to detach from certain situations in my life. It just works that way. You make a decision, commit to an **intention**, pay **attention** to it – and next thing you know, you're succeeding at what you set out to do. What a concept! My thought really does create my experience.

*"We speak into our words the Intelligence which we are,
and backed by that Greater Intelligence of the Universal Mind
our word becomes a law unto the thing for which it is spoken."*
Ernest Holmes

Your Word is the law of your life. Make the decision to live **Your Word** to the fullest. You get to do that. In fact, only you can do that.

- If you are in a group, share your thoughts with one another regarding **Your Word**. (Be mindful of your time allotment). No cross-talking.

Remember: It's okay to change **Your Word** throughout the week. Just commit to having one firmly in place before Week Two.

__Attention/Accountability__: Make an honest inventory of this week's directives and how well you accomplished them.

1. Did you pay **Attention** to Your **Word**?

2. Did you meditate and journal each morning?

3. Did you take three conscious moments to be mindful of **Your Word?**

4. Did you bring **Your Word** to mind before going to sleep?

If not, why not?

Don't be afraid to be brutally honest with your answers. It is only by acknowledging the facts and owning up to your own "story" that you can begin to rewrite it.

Quotes from Boot Camp

"My word is Acceptance. I don't know why that came to me, but I realized this week that in my world, as a child, everything had to be perfect or else

I wasn't safe. Accepting things as they are is hard for me. So, I think I'll stick with Acceptance."

"The word 'Authentic' came to me right away. I don't know what my life is supposed to be or what I'm supposed to be doing with it, but I have a feeling that there is an 'Authenticity' that doesn't need to be found, it needs to be uncovered. And I am SOOOOOO ready to uncover it."

"When I heard the word 'Felicity' come into my head I didn't know what it meant. That was weird. So, I looked it up. It means 'Intense Happiness.' That works for me. I'll stick with Felicity."

*"I need to stop looking at things as if I could succeed or fail. Wow. An hour into the 16 weeks and I'm already reaping the rewards. I don't work to succeed, I **AM** success. My word is RECEIVE!"*

"Since I got a lump in my throat when I tried to repeat the affirmation, 'I am fearless,' I am changing my word to FEARLESS! But I think it's really two words: FEAR LESS. Either way, that's where I'm headed."

That's where we're ALL headed!

Continue with this week's directives!

Keep Your Word!

Do the Work, LIVE THE RESULTS!

WEEK TWO
NO COMPLAINING

WEEK TWO

DAY ONE

**Meditation**: 10-minute minimum

Bring _**Your Word**_ into your meditation and allow your mind to surrender to the feeling that _**Your Word**_ brings forth. You are creating an "Energy Circle" around your life that connects you to how you understand and invest in _**Your Word**_. Let yourself feel this energy.

"I wait in perfect confidence for the WORD to fulfill itself in my life."
Ernest Holmes

**Communication**: What effect did _**Your Word**_ have on your life this week? One person, whose word was "release," noticed that just by focusing on the word, he was able to bring up a lot of B.S. that needed releasing. That's how it works. What we focus on becomes energized.

One thing that tends to happen when we choose a word is that our "story" starts to become vulnerable. Someone chooses the word "fearless" and then their "story" becomes obsolete. It has no more power. It doesn't serve a purpose to continue telling the "fear-driven" story anymore. Then it's time to write a new story – and title it "Fearless Me." After all, you are not your story. Your story is what you DO with who you are. And who you are is bigger than any story.

- Write your thoughts, without judgment, in your journal. Don't compete with yourself or anyone else for the most profound perceptions. Just tell it like it is. Don't try to be clever or creative. You already are those things. Start writing a new story.

- If you are in a group, share your thoughts (keeping mindful of your time allotment) from an impersonal perspective. You're not here to impress anyone, just understand yourself. No cross-talking. Opinions are useless. We are revealing Truth. Listen and you will hear it.

- Note: If for some reason you feel that **Your Word** needs to be changed, go for it. It's your decision. Just allow yourself to listen to your Intuition. You'll know exactly what to do. Don't allow yourself to get frustrated. Trust yourself.

Intention: This week's Intention is **_No Complaining._**

Have you ever noticed how much complaining goes on in the world? Perhaps you take part in this phenomenon. Complaining is something we do when we are actively avoiding the situation. The energy we put into complaining creates the "illusion" that we are actually doing something constructive. We're not! Let's make no mistake about it.

When we complain, we are just reinforcing the issue even further into the black whole of hopelessness. WE get into the "Blame Game," and we shirk responsibility for our part in whatever is going on. We focus our minds on the negative and therefore we are creating more of the same "Stuff."

Many times in Boot Camp, people will fight for their right to complain. "It helps me realize what's bothering me." "It's a way to let off steam." One woman told the group that, as a Jewish woman, "complaining was considered an Olympic sport." I told her that, by growing up in an Irish Catholic household, I couldn't imagine any other nationality getting the "gold" in complaining.

Regardless of your reasons, complaining is a waste of time. You cannot live life to the fullest when you are focusing on what is wrong. That doesn't mean that we don't acknowledge the problem. We do. But we focus our attention on the Truth of the situation, which is to know that behind the problem is the solution.

This week, you will NOT COMPLAIN about anything!

Sound impossible? It's not. It's actually quite freeing. The first time I gave this Intention, I was surrounded by students for the entire week and each time I started to complain about something (there truly is no delineation between teacher and student), one of my students would raise an eyebrow or smile in just "that way" that I would understand. Don't go there!

The most important thing to remember about complaining is this:

Complaining is a CHOICE!

Attention/Accountability: Paying attention to a behavior like complaining is an interesting thing. Most of us aren't aware of how much complaining we actually do. You may find that you don't really complain that much. Or you might find that you are one of the finalists at the Olympics. Regardless of how much you participate, the process is illuminating. The most important thing is for you to pay *Attention* to your complaining.

In the process of paying *Attention*, make no delineation between internal and external complaining. Listen to what you are thinking, as well as what actually makes it to your lips. A lot of destructive work occurs in the silence of our mind when it comes to complaining and blaming. It's a great first step to stop complaining verbally, but pay *attention* to what you are thinking as well.

Directives for the Week: Continue journaling each morning.

Each time you find yourself complaining, or catch yourself about to complain, ask yourself these questions:

1. When do I complain?

2. Why do I complain?

3. What am I avoiding in this moment?

Behind each complaint is something that needs to be known. It's very difficult to hear when the noise level of complaining is so high. Quieting the mind from the complaint allows us to know the Truth in any situation. So, as you "still" the complaint, replace it with the Truth (the higher thought).

This week, along with your morning journaling, just before you go to bed, write out how your day went with regard to complaining.

- How did I do?

- Did I pay attention to my complaining?

- Did I recognize what was behind the complaint?

- Did I replace the complaint with the Truth?

- Am I willing to do better tomorrow?

Remember: Today's Intention is tomorrow's success.

No Complaining!

WEEK TWO

DAY TWO

Meditation: Bring **Your Word** into your meditation. Remember to stay active. Activate your mind. Stay conscious of receiving what's coming through. Don't just zone out, step in!

> *"Happiness is the meaning and the purpose of life,*
> *the whole aim and end of human existence."*
> *Aristotle*

Communication: How does it feel to live without complaining? Are you good at it? Are you surprised by the amount of complaining you do? Is it less than you expected, more? When you reflect on what you've written in your journal, what do you think about yourself? What's behind the complaining? Do you know? If not, keep listening.

- Write about it. What's come up so far this week? Are you a complainer? Is the world around you complaining? If so, why do you think they are complaining to YOU? Don't judge yourself, just be willing to ask the questions and listen for the answers.

- If you are in a group, share your thoughts (keeping mindful of your time allotment). No cross-talking. Learn to listen without responding.

Intention: What comes up for most people is that they realize how much time they waste complaining about things they could just as easily have eliminated from their lives. We step into our power when we remove the clutter in our minds and free ourselves up to DO something constructive. Complaining creates clutter.

"I will not be as those who spend the day
In complaining of headache,
And the night in drinking the wine that gives it."
Johann Wolfgang von Goethe

What happens to us is that we become so steeped in a specific type of behavior that we aren't aware anymore of what is causing it. **WE** are causing it! We think it's the condition or person we are complaining about, but that's not the truth. We are at choice to either complain or know something better. But sometimes the complaint is out of our mouth before we are even conscious of it. It has become so ingrained in our "story" that it's on autopilot.

I notice that I complain most when I'm not happy. And the complaining is usually not even related to what I'm not happy about. Ever notice that? When I'm not living the life I want, everything seems wrong and it's easier to complain about the clogged sink than get involved with why I'm in a situation I don't like.

One Boot Camper said that when he stopped complaining, his energy shifted from self-destruction to self-creation. What he was doing was clearing the space for creativity to inhabit his mind.

"If you're complaining, you're not resolving anything!"

So how did it go these past few days?

Attention/Accountability: Make an inventory of this week's directives and how well you accomplished them.

   1. Did you meditate and journal each morning?

   2. Did you really pay ***ATTENTION*** to your complaining by asking the questions provided whenever you caught yourself "in the act?"

3. Did you conclude each day with an assessment of how you did?

If not, why not? Keep on yourself as you go through this process. Notice whether or not you keep promises you make to yourself. If we lack the respect to follow through on what we Intend, it is something to reflect on.

This is what is meant by Self-Respect!

For the remainder of this week, see what gets your **attention,** and then pay **attention**. That's why you're here.

Quotes from Boot Camp

"This is really frustrating. I thought I was someone who didn't complain much. I guess it's all relative to what you think of as 'much.' Now it feels like even a little is too much."

"I don't know about the rest of you, but the gold medal is mine."

"I know one thing. Something has to give because I can't keep doing it this way. I'm just gonna put my complaints under my pillow and let the pillow fairy handle it."

"What do you do when you realize that all of your friends are complainers? I like my energy circle, but I don't want to be in there alone."

"I've noticed that there's always a chain reaction when I complain."

"Sometimes I feel like I go from kvetch to kvetch, crisis to crisis. This no complaining thing is exhausting."

"I realized that 'My Story' is just one big complaint!"

"I guess on one level, there really isn't anything to complain about."

Continue with this week's directives!

No Complaining!

Do the work ... LIVE THE RESULTS!

WEEK THREE EXPECTATIONS

WEEK THREE

DAY ONE

Meditation: 10-minute minimum

Clearing your life of complaining has allowed you to build on your Energy Circle. Knowing the Truth, rather than focusing solely on the facts, is a way of life that transcends chaos and brings harmony. It allows for Inner Peace. Bring these words into your meditation.

> *"In Truth, to attain to interior peace,*
> *one must be willing to pass through the contrary to peace."*
> *Swami Brahmananda*

"Passing through the contrary" is refusing to allow things like complaints to take up residence in our minds. Complaining is the contrary. Without it cluttering up our minds, we are free to create what it is we wish to experience – peace of mind.

Communication: How has not complaining changed your life? Has it? Are you willing to continue this until it becomes second nature? If not, why? Does it feel natural to complain, or is it starting to feel natural **NOT** to complain? Do you hear the complaints when they're internal and perhaps not spoken? Those are deadly.

One Boot Camper put it this way: "I don't have to take things personally, but I also don't have to take things as they are."

Not complaining doesn't mean that we lie down in the middle of the world and get run over. Eliminating the complaint clears away the B.S. and allows us to see things clearly. We can make the choice to change what we don't like, what isn't useful, what doesn't serve us, into something that brings joy, is beneficial and serves our higher good. Let's face it, the more we complain, the more we find things to complain about. It's like putting in an order for "more of the same." And to top it off, no one looks good complaining. It does terrible things to the face.

Am I complaining because of something "out there," or is my complaining causing what's happening "out there" to land on my doorstep? We know the answer. STOP COMPLAINING!

One Boot Camper said that the greatest gift of No Complaining Week was the awareness. By paying attention to our complaining, we get to recognize patterns, write them down and step into the solution.

Sometimes we think complaining is funny. It's all part of our sense of humor. That might be the case, and many comedians have made a career out of complaining – just look at Rodney Dangerfield! But there's a difference between humor for humor's sake and genuine complaining disguised as humor. If you really take the time to listen, you'll hear the difference.

Another thing about complaining, it removes us from the present moment. Regardless of what you are complaining about, you are relegating yourself to something in the past.

Complaining conjures up the PAST
and catapults us into a fractured future.

Here's what I've come to realize: conscious, directed thinking eliminates complaining. Most of what we complain about is fear-based. If we are consciously creating our experience by being present and paying **attention** to what we are thinking, we step out of fear and into that which moves us forward. We break old habits and create new practices.

One Boot Camper put it this way: "Holy SHIT! This 'no complaining' directive has been mind-blowing. I think I've been on a 'maintenance' program for a long time and now, with Mental Muscle, I'm working out again, lifting heavier weights, sweating more. I'm moving from maintenance to spiritual growth. Who knew not complaining would be so eye opening?"

What did you find this week? Did you do the directive to the best of your ability? Were you accountable to yourself? Did you pay **attention**? Are you sweating? Are you maintaining, or are you growing?

- Take a look at your journal, focusing on what you wrote each night during your week of no complaining. Write a paragraph or two explaining what you experienced, learned and decided based on your work.

- If you are in a group, share your thoughts (keeping mindful of your time allotment). No cross-talking.

One more thing before we leave this week: In answer to the person who asked what to do when all of your friends seem to be complainers, you will find that, as you stop complaining, others around you will follow suit. It's hard to complain when there's no one to complain to. And if that doesn't work, you will most likely find a new group of friends.

**Intention**: This week's Intention is _**Expectancy.**_

Believe it or not, you are expecting something to happen in your life right now in this very moment. All of us have expectations that are either buried, unconscious or rote. Add them to our conscious expectations, and you have the motor that fuels our forward momentum.

> _"We must learn to reawaken and keep ourselves awake,_
> _not by mechanical aid, but by an infinite expectation of the dawn."_
> _Henry David Thoreau_

As Thoreau so eloquently put it, we must always expect the dawn of a new idea, a new thought, and a new realization. When you go to sleep at night, don't you expect to wake to another day? If you don't, take a look at that. We all expect the sun to rise the next morning. So why is it that we have to work so hard to expect the Truth to come forth in the midst of a dark reality? This difficulty is something we have learned. And we can relearn it! We can refocus our expectations to create richer, fuller, and more successful lives.

When you expect something to happen, truly expect it, IT HAPPENS!

Expect the Good! What's the alternative?

During one Boot Camp session, it became clear that most people confuse expectation with hope. Hope is good – it's better than despair. But it's not strong enough to create what you want. Expectancy leaves no room for failure. Hope depends on others. Expectancy realizes that what you are focused on will ultimately reveal itself as the byproduct of your very **attention** to it.

This week you will focus on EXPECTANCY!

Get in touch with what you actually are expecting right at this moment. Are you expecting to have a great week? Are you expecting to win the lottery? (Does anyone *really* expect to win the lottery?) Do you expect things to get better? Do you expect this Boot Camp to be a changing force in your life? What are you expecting from the world? What are you expecting from your career? What are you expecting from the economy? It's important for you to know the answer to these questions because it relates to all areas of your life.

I expect only that which is GOOD!

Once again, let me be very clear that expectation is *not* hope. Hope leaves room for failure. It creates the illusion that something else might be at play other than the power of your own mind. That is not the case.

Expectancy leaves no room for failure.
Hope depends on others.

__Attention/Accountability__: In every situation there is an expectancy. Most of the time it is unspoken, but it's there. Your job this week is to continually check in with yourself and see what the expectation is. Will dinner with so-and-so be boring or fun? Will this job interview turn into something, or will it be like all the others? What are you expecting it to be? That's what it will be. Pay *attention* and you will see how you are creating your experience through your expectations.

Another thing to pay close **attention** to is whether your expectations are your own. Chances are there are some expectations left over from the past or from well-intentioned people in your life. Your job is to get to the core of your **OWN** expectations.

__Directives for the Week__: Pay *Attention* to what you are expecting.

When you wake up, take a moment and see what you are expecting for your day. Write it down. Then ask yourself the following questions:

    1. Am I being honest with myself?

    2. Is this what I wish to experience?

    3. What would be the most productive expectation for my day?

Remember: There is no limit to what you can expect. Only you can limit yourself. And, if you read this and hear this voice inside your head saying, "My life is limited and there's nothing I can do about it," tell yourself **ENOUGH!**

The only reason your life is limited is because that is what you are expecting. You were probably taught to expect that.

I can clearly hear my mother telling me, "Don't expect too much and you won't be disappointed." She meant well and I know she was trying to protect me. After all, I wanted to be a Broadway star. And, as my grandmother used to say, "There's a lot of rejection in the acting world." Clearly, my mother got it from her mother and hers before her.

Looking back, I wondered how any of them knew anything about the rejection of actors. None of them were in the "business."

Just so you know, I starred in my first Broadway show when I was 25. Clearly, I expected it!

This week, along with your morning journaling, before you go to bed, write out how your day went with regard to expectancy.

- Did what I expected play out? If not, what changed?

- Did I pay **attention** to what I was expecting in each interaction?

- Am I beginning to expose expectations that are old and useless? If yes, make a list.

- Are my expectations my own, or are they handed down from the past?

I expect only that which is GOOD!

WEEK THREE

DAY TWO

Meditation: As you enter meditation this day, bring with you an expectancy of knowing more, allowing more, hearing more. Instruct your mind to release any unwanted thoughts, ideas or images. Then drift into the "silence" to commune with your True Self.

> *"In the attitude of silence the soul finds the path in a clearer light, and what is elusive and deceptive resolves itself into crystal clearness."*
> *Mahatma Gandhi*

If you begin with an attitude of expectancy, whatever you expect will, as Gandhi wrote, "find the path in a clearer light."

Communication: Thinking back to the start of this week, how did you expect it to go? Did it live up to your expectations? Were you able to redirect specific expectations to bring about a more desirable result? Were you surprised at what types of expectations you already had in place? Did you notice how you reacted to others' expectations of you?

Being as clear and honest as possible, let yourself speak aloud your thoughts from the past couple of days.

You can read what you wrote each night as a prelude and then continue by allowing your thoughts to pour out at random – this is not a performance, but a releasing. Be brutally honest. And if you have trouble with this directive, push your way through your resistance. Let yourself hear your own voice. It is a very freeing thing to speak out with abandon.

- Now, jot down whatever sticks out in your mind about what you just said.

- If you are in a group, share your thoughts (keeping mindful of your time allotment). No cross-talking. Allow your mind to release whatever thoughts you have about the directives. Be brutally honest.

Intention: Very often during Expectation Week, a person may come face-to-face with a reluctance to expect too much. There is something within that keeps a lid on just how much good any of us can expect. One person wrote, "I cower if I get too happy, too big, too in alignment. I don't want to seem like I'm a show-off." Well, guess what? No one has more or less of anything than anyone else. We all have exactly the same right to unlimited good, prosperity, love, opportunity, health. Whatever we desire is already fully available for everyone equally. So, the idea of not "showing off" for fear of someone feeling "less" is counterproductive. Nothing good comes from playing small. Let me repeat that:

NOTHING GOOD COMES FROM PLAYING SMALL!

The only thing that comes from not living up to our potential is a life half-lived or worse, barely lived. One Boot Camper put it perfectly:

"I'm tired of holding back my bloom. It's getting tight in here."

Attention/Accountability: Make an inventory of the directives and how well you accomplished them.

1. Did you meditate and journal each morning?

2. Did you pay ***ATTENTION*** to what you were expecting?

3. Did you conclude each day with an assessment of how you did?

If not, why not?

By now, you have a pretty clear indication of what to expect with regard to Boot Camp. If you are one of those people who start out strong and then lose interest or peter out at the finish line, ***EXPECT MORE OF YOURSELF!*** No one is going to do it for you. If you expect success, you have to do what it takes to succeed.

Remember: **You** are the only one who can make a difference in your life! There may be others who inspire, but you alone will either make use of or toss aside what they have to offer. It's all up to **you**.

This is what is meant by Self-Reliant!

Quotes from Boot Camp

"Yesterday I realized that I don't expect much from my life considering who I am. When I heard this in my head I thought, WHAT? Actually, I thought something else, but I'm being polite."

"Someone once told me, 'Hope for the best, prepare for the worst.' I don't remember who it was, but I'm pissed off because that's how I live my life."

"I've noticed that my life is about 'extremes.' I expect the highs, and therefore I expect the lows. And that's what I get, the highs and lows."

"I wait until something happens to realize that it's what I expected to happen. Time to put the expectation before the experience."

Put the expectation BEFORE the experience!

"There's been an umbrella in my car for many years ... on many levels. I guess I'm expecting a lot of rain, literally and figuratively."

Use this affirmation throughout the week: ***"My success is non-negotiable!"***

Continue with this week's directives!

Do the work ... LIVE THE RESULTS!

WEEK FOUR
BELIEF

WEEK FOUR

DAY ONE

Meditation: 10-minute minimum. Use the following affirmation to focus your ***intention*** as you meditate.

I expect only GOOD!

Repeat this to yourself, noticing how it makes you feel. Do you believe it, or is it something you would *like* to believe? Allow the words to resonate within the silence of your meditation. If at any time you feel yourself drifting, just repeat the affirmation and continue.

Communication: How did your week go? Was it what you expected? Were you able to pinpoint expectations within each experience? Did you notice expectations left over from the past? Are you still living expectations that have expired? What are your global expectations (overall expectancies that you carry with you, coloring life a certain shade of half-empty/half-full)? Are there any expectations at play that aren't yours, but left over from other people in your life?

Were you completely honest with yourself? When you began your day, did you find it easy to identify what you were expecting? How did it feel refocusing your energy to expect what you wanted? When you did your end-of-day assessment, were there any realizations that were surprising? Did you do the work?

Last week, you were asked to allow yourself a free flow of thought regarding your expectations of life. Letting your thoughts fly from your consciousness into the ether of audible sound is a freeing experience (if you give yourself over to it). How did it feel for you?

The overall directive was to take your waking thoughts and discover what we were expecting for the day. If you didn't like what you were expecting, you were directed to change the expectation. How did that go? Did it come easy? Are your expectations accessible and clear? Are there expectations, core expectations, that have control of your day-to-day existence? Does it change things when you decide to expect only the **GOOD**?

- Looking back over this week, rereading your nightly journaling and exploring the seven-day journey, write down your perceptions.

- Make a special effort to uncover expectations that are placed upon you from outside of yourself.

- If you are in a group, share your thoughts (keeping mindful of your time allotment). No cross-talking, and keep notes on what resonates with you.

One of the benefits of journaling during this process is to remember realizations you won't want to forget. It is so easy to slip back into old ways of thinking. Having a journal to go back and reread gives you the opportunity to rediscover again and again the truth of who you are.

Intention: This week's Intention is **_Belief._**

*Behind every expectation is the **BELIEF** that it will or will not happen*

One Easter, I remember sitting on the floor of our living room watching Mary Martin fly across our "modern" black-and-white television screen as Peter Pan. (Does it even seem possible that there was actually black-and-white television in our lifetime?) At one point, she looked out from her captive box and asked us to say: "I do believe in fairies." This was so that Tinkerbell would live. I can tell you that it never crossed my mind to not believe in fairies. Cynicism would come much later.

Years later, my 9-year-old son announced that he no longer believed in the Easter Bunny. He said he knew it was just a guy dressed up in a bunny costume. For him, it no longer made any sense. So, I asked him about Santa Claus, and he looked me straight in the eyes and said, "Dad, of course there's a Santa Claus, I'm not that stupid." I was relieved.

Behind every expectation is the belief that it will or will not happen. If you have found it difficult to direct your expectations, that's because your belief system isn't creating the foundation for this new expectation. If you believe something will happen, you then expect it to happen, and it happens! It's the belief that informs the thought that informs the expectancy. Let me repeat that:

Belief informs the Thought that informs the Expectancy.

We each have a set of beliefs that we use as we navigate life. There was a time when the belief that the world was flat kept humankind from going too far in any one direction for fear of falling off the Earth. I think we still have that belief somewhere embedded in our collective consciousness. We somehow believe in failure, so we are conscious not to make our endeavors too vast. We believe that there's not enough money in the world for everyone, so we stick to a "fixed income" that is safe. We believe that we can be hurt if we love too deeply, so we keep our affections on the surface, protecting our intimate feelings. We believe a lot of things that keep us from falling off the Earth. But we are made of Heaven, not Earth.

> *"Our deepest fear is not that we are inadequate.*
> *Our deepest fear is that we are powerful beyond measure."*
> *Marianne Williamson*

It is our responsibility to not buy into things such as lack, disease, fear, or failure. We must turn our "deepest fear" into our deepest belief. It must become a matter of faith, not merely a matter of fact. And it all starts with your belief about yourself. Who are you?

What do you believe about yourself? When you look in the mirror, who do you see? If you look around at your life, what you have accomplished, what you have created, your successes, your failures, your relationships, you will find tangible proof for what you have believed up to this point.

Whether or not you like what you see doesn't matter. The great news is that you can change your beliefs, change your thinking, and create new expectancy. What you are looking at, in this moment, does not have to be what you see tomorrow, or even in the next moment.

One Boot Camper said: "I liken belief to an escalator. You keep taking one step after another and there's always another one to place your foot on."

If you can believe in an escalator, why not try believing in the power of your own mind? Your mind can uproot any false belief and plant another one that you choose to cultivate. Belief is a **Choice!**

I choose to create a belief system that works for me!

At this point during Boot Camp, I ask the participants to give me one thing they believe without any doubt. Here are some of the things they've said:

"I believe that I am on the right path."
"I believe in kindness."
"I believe there is a God."
"I believe my belief creates my experience."
"I believe that I will survive at all costs."
"I believe that I have to do things to make people like me."
"I believe it's never too late to start over."
"I believe that people are basically good."
"I believe that my cup is half full. But I want to believe that it is completely full. Forget the empty part altogether."
"I believe that I'm starting to believe."

What is your one belief?

Attention/Accountability: When we pay attention to our behavior, we begin to notice patterns. These patterns are being created by our beliefs. Our core beliefs are those things that we have developed since birth. We go through stages of belief. First, we inherit the beliefs of our parents or influential adults in our lives. We then often abandon those beliefs to search for our own individual beliefs. As we mature, we develop beliefs based on experience. These beliefs are now embedded in our personality, and life patterns develop based on what we have accepted as our belief system.

Our job this week is to recognize our core beliefs and make a conscious decision as to whether or not they are servicing us. For instance, I used to believe that a hole in my heart prohibited me from playing sports. I was told this. I believed this. Until one day, I decided to take matters into my own hands. I went and joined the crew team at my college. I made varsity lightweight and never looked back.

Note: Years later, when I was dancing on Broadway as Riff in "West Side Story," I was asked to see a specialist to make sure I wasn't exacerbating the hole in my heart. **IT WAS GONE!** I still have a murmur, but I kind of like the extra beat – so I'm okay with that.

"It is done unto you as you believe."
Matthew 9:29

Directives for the Week: On a regular daily basis, ask yourself, "***What do I believe?***" More importantly, make sure you know ***WHY*** you believe what you believe.

Continue with your morning journal. Only this week, as you wake up, ask yourself the following questions:

1. Name one thing I definitely believe.

2. Why do I believe it?

3. Do I wish to continue believing this thing?

4. If I don't wish to believe it, what can I replace it with?

Remember: You get to decide what you believe. If there are beliefs left over from "Your Story," and you don't have a need for them anymore, dump them. It's time to make room for beliefs that will take you where you want to go.

I choose to create a Belief System that works for me!

WEEK FOUR

DAY TWO

**Meditation**: 10-minute minimum. Read the following and allow your mind to expand beyond the ideas into the meaning.

> _There is a Truth within, an Infinite Truth, that washes across the_
> _Universe_
> _with clarity and purpose. A knowing so pure and intimate,_
> _it speaks beyond words into the deepest feeling of the soul._
> _There, in the face of such Truth you will find your Higher Self._

**Communication**: Spending a week analyzing your beliefs is a bold step into knowing yourself from the inside out. As you question the reasons for these beliefs to even have a presence in your life, you are beginning to understand how your life has evolved and why life is the way it is. More importantly, you are learning the future is yours to create, regardless of anything that has happened in your lifetime.

Building a foundation of beliefs that empower you to succeed is the goal here and it is certain to be achieved. How does this make you feel?

- Make a list of the beliefs that have come up this week.

- What beliefs have you decided to embrace?

- What beliefs are you ready to discard?

- If you are in a group, share your thoughts (keeping mindful of your time allotment). No cross-talking. Own up to beliefs that are hard to shake.

Remember: The first step to succeeding at anything is a willingness to do the work. If you find yourself frustrated by beliefs that you feel you can't shake, just tell yourself you are **_willing_** to shake them. That **intention** alone will create a breakthrough.

Intention: It's not easy knowing what you believe, is it? As one person put it, "it's an interesting journey of half-beliefs/sub-beliefs." It's one thing to know that we can change our world. It's another to DO IT. If I know that I can, why don't I? The difference between CAN and DO lies in our beliefs.

At this point, it is important to state that we CAN change our beliefs. We CAN move from one belief to a stronger belief. It's all part of our Spiritual Practice. The more we talk to ourselves from a place of Truth and refuse to focus on conditions, the more strength we are adding to our Belief System. It is imperative that we stay on course and not allow anything to distract us from what we know.

In Belief, there is no room for doubt!

To be clear, you cannot believe something and doubt it simultaneously. You are always either doing one thing or the other. The question is, which are you allowing to get your **attention**? You get to choose. Which one will it be? Negative beliefs have a way of digging in and staying around long after the party is over. They become so comfortable that they appear to be blood related. They aren't. Any belief that doesn't support, nurture and honor your True Self needs to be eradicated. NOW!

As one Boot Camper put it, "It's always easy to talk about self-worth, but *actually facing* my beliefs about my self-worth? That's a different story." It's time to stop talking about it and actually face the truth about it.

You were born to believe in yourself fully, fearlessly, vibrantly and completely.

Attention/Accountability: Make an inventory of the directives and how well you accomplished them.

1. Did you meditate and journal each morning?

2. Did you pay ***ATTENTION*** to the beliefs as they arose?

3. Did you conclude each day with an assessment of how you did?

If not, why not?

Don't allow excuses to give you a way out. Excuses are just another name for failure. If you want to find an excuse, you will. An excuse is just a reason for why you aren't doing the work. If you want to succeed, you won't have time for excuses.

Quotes from Boot Camp

"Is it even possible that I don't believe in myself? Unfortunately, I think it is."

"I'm beginning to believe that there are beliefs I'm not even aware of that are playing games with me."

"Belief and Faith and Religion all get mixed up for me. And I don't like talking about God. I need something real to believe in."

"I believe(d) that my body is damaged and can never be as fit and healthy as I'd like it to be. Enough of that B.S.!"

"Today, right here in this room, I believe that things can be different from what they have been."

"I still don't know what I believe. But I am willing to figure it out. That's how it works, right?"

"I feel like I should have a garage sale given the number of beliefs I'm ready to throw away. But I don't really want anyone else to buy them either."

Continue with this week's directives!

Believe you can ... and you will!

Do the work ... LIVE THE RESULTS!

WEEK FIVE
BE PRESENT

Meditation: 10-minute minimum

The goal in meditation should be to connect to the energy of life, in whatever way works best for you. When you connect with an inner knowing, you are able to tap into your authentic self. From a clear belief in who you are, you can recognize the limitless possibilities that stretch before you.

> *"Our beliefs set the limit of our demonstration of*
> *a principle which, of Itself,*
> *is without limit. It is ready to fill everything because it is infinite.*
> *It is entirely a question of our receptivity."*
> *Ernest Holmes*

As you meditate, invite your mind to relax and surrender to the quantum field of possibility all around you. Allow the following words to resonate with you in whatever way feels right. Use it as a suggestion, a springboard to whatever comes next. Empty your mind and feel it fill up with a vibrant, peaceful energy.

> *"You are never alone or helpless.*
> *The force that guides the stars guides you too."*
> *Shrii Shrii Anandamurti*

Communication: Last week I asked you who you believed yourself to be. The reason for that is simple. Belief is tied to self-worth. There is a Spiritual worth to all of humankind. In that place of Truth, we are all perfect, complete expressions of infinite good.

However, when we base our self-worth on the relative facts and not the Universal Truth that life is constantly expanding and moving, we quite often come up short. To make matters worse, we turn this acceptance of the facts into a belief.

What we wind up doing is bouncing back and forth from belief to belief. It becomes an endless circle of believing what we see and creating more of the same, instead of believing the Truth and creating something better.

What beliefs came up this week? Have you been journaling, meditating, doing the work? If you're doing the work, you're feeling the results. One Boot Camper said, "I'm developing so much Mental Muscle that I need a back brace to hold my head up." Another said, "One of my beliefs is (was) 'I'll know it when I see it.' I'm ready to believe that 'I'll see it when I know it.'"

During one of our sessions, someone told the story of how baby elephants are trained for a life in captivity by attaching a six-foot chain around one of their legs and shackling them to a stake. They learn to walk round and round the stake and never realize that they are strong enough to break free. Even after they grow big and powerful, they are tied to their earliest belief that they are destined to stay shackled.

What limiting beliefs are keeping you shackled to a life of habits and excuses.

- Write out the list of beliefs from your weekly journal, continuing on from Day Two of last week. How do they stack up? Can you see where your life is headed based on your current beliefs?

- Now make a list of the beliefs you have decided to cultivate. Can you see how beliefs are tied to self-worth and to the manifestation of your desires?

- Write out a description of who you believe yourself to be. Do this from a spiritual understanding of who you are, not based on the facts of your life. Those are just the results of how you used who you are to create the life you've lived thus far. If it feels dishonest, so what? All you need to know is that regardless of how it feels, it is the Truth! Read it out loud to yourself and hear it as the Truth.

- If you are in a group, read aloud your description of yourself. Discuss the way it makes you feel reading this out loud in front of people. Keep mindful of your time allotment. No cross-talking, and keep notes on what resonates with you.

Descriptions from past Boot Campers:

"I am capable, stable, financially secure and unstoppable!"
"I am tall, dark and handsome ... on a spiritual plane."
"I am compassion, love, responsibility, self-awareness, integrity, faith and more than I could have ever imagined. The difference is, now I imagine!"
"I am POSSIBLE!"
"Five foot three and yet as tall as an oak tree."
"I think I want to stop the description right after I AM. That says it all."

Intention: This week's Intention is **Be Present.**

Now this might seem like an easy thing to do, **Be Present**, but how many times have you driven somewhere and suddenly realized that you don't remember getting where you are? What was I thinking these past few minutes? Where was I? My body's here but my mind is miles away.

Ever had someone talk to you and tune them out? Ever gotten bored by something you were doing and, while you continued doing it, you left the building and thought about something, ANYTHING else?

Once while I was performing in **42nd Street** (as the tap-dancing juvenile, Billy Lawlor), I was in front of an audience of 2,800 people, tapping away on top of a giant dime. I had been performing in the show for more than a year and, by this point, I was on autopilot. I started thinking about where I was going to have dinner that night after the show. All of a sudden, the number was over, people were applauding, and I couldn't remember which number I had just finished. I had to look down to see what I was wearing to figure out where I was. You'd have thought the dime would have given me a hint. Scary! That was *NOT* being present.

> *"By watching the mechanics of the mind,*
> *you step out of its resistance patterns,*
> *and you can then allow the present moment to be."*
> Eckhart Tolle

The importance of being present cannot be overstated. Our culture is so committed to living in the future, we seldom even taste our food anymore. Moments in time are passing us by and we're the poorer for it. We're trying so hard to "get somewhere" that we don't appreciate the beauty of where we are. And the more important question is, where are we trying to go? As if some destination "out there" is better than where we are. The only destination is the one we've already arrived at. We just need to decide to be here in the now.

Years ago, when my daughter was only 5 or 6, Nora asked me to come outside and look at a flower she found. I was busy at the time doing something that I'm sure was of monumental importance. She smiled and ran back out to look at the flower. From the window, I could see her staring at this flower with such delight.

I got up, put my work down and went out to join her. She was so excited to show me this flower that had only bloomed that morning. "It wasn't there yesterday and here it is today," she said in amazement. I will always remember that moment. And I might have missed it if I hadn't decided to listen to my child's request. Sometimes we just need to listen to what's being asked of us.

During one Boot Camp, I realized that being present forces us to live Intuitively. If we persist on living in the moment, we open the floodgates to a world of quantum energy. It is the most authentic of worlds when we bring our *Attention* to the present moment. There is a power unparalleled, waiting to be tapped and it's only found in the **Present**.

> *"Do not dwell in the past, do not dream of the future, concentrate the mind on the present moment."*
> *Buddha*

Attention/Accountability: In order to live in the present, you must bring your *Attention* into every situation. You must be vigilant in focusing your mind and using the strength of your mental muscle to keep it focused.

Directives for the Week: Continue with your morning journal and meditation. Follow your thoughts and write them down. Don't allow your mind to drift without following it. Stay present.

During the week, be aware of when you are present and when you are not. When you catch yourself drifting away, ask yourself what it is you are stepping away from. What are you avoiding? This can be very enlightening. Make notes on those times and circumstances when you "phone it in."

- This week, you will take one hour a day to do something that fills you from within. Something that you enjoy. A break from your usual schedule. If you normally go for a jog in the morning, insist on being present throughout. Take a specific hour for yourself where you will **Be Present** for the entire time doing something you like doing.

Some ideas from previous Boot Campers: *Roller skating, hiking, a trip to the museum, a needlepoint class, going to the movies, pole dancing (really), shooting hoops, playing the piano.*

Remember: Only you know what makes you blissful, what fills you up. It's up to you to take the time to honor yourself by showing up. Don't let this week slide by without giving yourself the present of **Being Present.** You might miss the most wonderful flower, or a chance to see delight in the eyes of a child. You might miss a moment that is truly "amazing."

"We should erase the thoughts of yesterday
that would rob us of today's happiness!"
Ernest Holmes

There's a reason they call it ... THE PRESENT!

WEEK FIVE

DAY TWO

__Meditation__: 10-minute minimum

Look around and connect to what you see. Take it in. Let it become part of you. Feel the Oneness we all share with the entire Universe. Now, touch your fingers together and connect with your body. Feel the energy circle surrounding you and focus on that energy. In this moment, having expanded your awareness to the wholeness of the Universe, consciously direct your focus to your individual self.

Repeat the following, allowing the final **I** to take you into the silence.

I AM HERE

I AM HERE

I AM

I AM

I

I

__Communication__: How does it feel ***Being Present*** in each moment? What things took you out of the moment and caused you to either look back or race forward? Was it difficult to stay present in conversations with others? Did you notice others when they weren't being present, moving through life by rote or checking out? What things caused you to check out?

- Take a moment here to write about it.

- Very often, when we practice the presence, we become aware of our connection to everything around us. The intimate details of a tree somehow seem to resonate on a deeper level. The sounds of the ocean become familiar, as if they are emanating from our very soul. Reflect on the past few days and notate any shifts in attitude, feeling or perception. Are you happier, more energetic? Does the world seem larger?

- Make a list of the things you did during your hour of personal time. Write down the way those things made you feel.

- If you are in a group, share your thoughts, your feelings, and your perceptions. Don't be worried about how they are being heard. Just stay present and allow yourself to explore. Keep mindful of your time allotment. No cross-talking.

Intention: There comes a time when the unexplainable shifts into the understandable. **Being Present** is a catalyst for such a shift. We might not have the exact words for what we perceive, but words can only take us so far. There is that within each of us that goes beyond the words, beyond the knowledge, beyond the feeling.

The other day while I was in the middle of taking a shower, I realized that I had no conscious memory of the previous five minutes. I knew that I'd washed my hair, or had I? I knew there as soap on the washcloth, but the actual time seemed to be lost. I immediately remembered that it was "Be Present" week and stopped. I focused my **Attention** on the water coming from the shower head, its warmth, the scent of the soap (lavender) and the feeling of the water hitting my shoulders. In an instant I was catapulted into the present moment and a surge of energy wafted over my entire being. Just by Being Present! That is the intention here. To be **AWAKE** and to live from that **ALIVENESS!**

Attention/Accountability:

1. Did you meditate and journal each morning?

2. Did you take the hour each day for yourself?

3. Did you make notes of when and why you detached from the present?

If not, why not?

By now I would expect you to answer all questions in the affirmative. If, for whatever reason you answered in the negative, make a better effort. Remember: If you don't think you're worth the effort, who will?

Quotes from Boot Camp

"Spiritual Practice really brings up the GUNK. And Being Present, I can't pretend it isn't there."

"Authenticity can be scary! I think that's why sometimes I run away into the hinterlands of my mind."

"Sometimes it's all hurry up and make it happen. Make WHAT happen? I don't even know anymore; I'm just hurrying up."

"Today I listened to Pink Floyd's 'Dark Side of the Moon' from beginning to end. What an hour!"

"Could it be that I have been depressed, stuck and shackled by my own beliefs for some time and not even known it? WOW! What an eye opener. No wonder I don't like being present."

"I'm starting to look within for answers I've always sought outside of myself. I guess if I'm here I might as well start with me."

"Coming up with things to do for my hour was like visiting a Jewish deli. Everything was on the menu and the portions were huge. I should live like this all the time."

"I haven't taken a nap since I was a child. This week I've taken naps every day as part of my hour. I wake up extremely present. What a present."

Continue with this week's directives!

I keep My Word and stay <u>AWAKE</u> in the moment!

Do the work ... LIVE THE RESULTS!

WEEK SIX
PATIENCE

WEEK SIX

DAY ONE

Meditation: 10-minute minimum

As you prepare for today's meditation, consider the words of Dr. Ernest Holmes:

> *"I stand in the midst of eternal opportunity,*
> *which is forever presenting me with the evidence of its full expression.*
> *I am joy, peace and happiness.*
> *I radiate Life, I am Life.*
> *There is but one Life and that Life is my life now!"*

In the present moment, Life is pouring Itself through you on every level. Take this time to experience this Life-affirming energy.

Communication: Many of us have not lived our lives fully present. We always found ways to escape into tomorrow or drift back into yesterday. Today was something that we needed to "get through." In the famous words of Scarlet O'Hara, "I'll think about it tomorrow." And then it was tomorrow, presenting itself with pretty much the same scenario. Only now, we're creating a "dread cycle" where we build up more fear and anxiety around something than it ever warranted.

Being present allows us to take things as they come and know the Truth about them, based on our knowledge that it is all Spirit. In a precious split second, you can turn your life around merely by becoming present, remembering who you are and designing your life from the infinite possibilities that are always there to be tapped into.

One person noted that she recognized a mega multi-tasking habit. In Carl Honoré's book, "In Praise of Slowness," he writes that multi-tasking is the enemy of efficiency. When we split our focus over several things, we are also splitting the energy. And while it might seem like we get more things done in a day faster, in reality, we don't. The power is in being fully present with each task. Staying present actually gives me more time in my day. And stopping the endless "to do" list chattering in my head also gives me more time to actually get some of my tasks done. Now I do them one at a time, staying present and accomplishing more.

In order for you to communicate this week's journey into the present, and in order for you to stay fully present as you sift through the past, try this exercise:

- Close your eyes and listen to the sounds of the room.

- Take a deep breath and breathe in the smells.

- Touch your fingertips gently to the sides of your face.

- Now move your hands away from your face and slowly open your eyes.

When you feel ready, begin to journal your experience with this week's directive.

How did it feel staying present? Did you take the time to check-in during the day to determine if you were present or not? What excuses did you unearth? What takes you away from being present? What was it like taking an HOUR a day to focus on being present in your life, doing what you wanted to do? Did you take the hour EVERY DAY? Is this something that resonates with you, or is it not that important? And if it wasn't that important for you to take time for yourself, why wasn't it?

As you begin to write, if you feel yourself drifting into your memories, go back to the top of the exercise. Close your eyes and listen to the sounds of the room. Continue through the steps until you are present again. Then go back to writing. Allow yourself to do this as often as you like throughout your journaling.

- If you are in a group, do this exercise together. Then begin sharing your week with the group, keeping mindful of your time allotment. No cross-talking, but feel free to continue the "present" exercise throughout the Communication part of Boot Camp.

Intention: This week's Intention is **Patience.**

True Patience is Knowing!

I have to admit that I have not always been a patient man. I was one of those people who never read the directions, because it took too long and I was certain that I could get it done faster if I just "did it." The truth is, I usually had to go back and read the directions anyway. So how does that link up to *Knowing?*

Knowing that Life is always working as planned, and that there is good in everything, takes the impatience out of living. I'm not in a hurry, because I like where I am. I'm not trying to "get" somewhere else. I am always where it is best for me to be. There is a definite science behind the idea of being present in the moment in order to focus our energy on what we WANT to expand. So, as I Believe that my life is Good, it is! As I stay in the present, and know the truth about who and what I am, I AM. And there isn't any reason for me to be impatient given what I know. But I have to keep knowing it on a daily basis.

Impatience is a SHOULD ...
Patience is an I AM.

Life is filled with 'SHOULDS.' I should do this today, but I'd rather do that. I should have done this yesterday, but I didn't, I did that other thing. I REALLY should do this now but instead I think I'll do something else. I should change that about me. Why? Clearly, the problem here is that what you think you should do, you don't want to do. Ever try to make a child put on a sweater when they're not cold? I did. It didn't go well. You know why? SHE WASN'T COLD! I learned that lesson quickly as the father of twin 2-year-olds. Children don't live in the world of "shoulds." They just live in the present moment.

Patience comes when a person is present in his or her life and is in touch with their individual purpose. Patience isn't slowness. On the contrary, it is vibrant with energy and passion. When I am patient I have the ability to accomplish anything and everything.

Patience is being connected to your True Self.

Attention/Accountability: Pay **attention** this week to how you work with patience. Notice when you have patience and when you don't. There's a reason for both scenarios. Pay attention to what comes before a loss of patience and what follows. You'll be amazed at the effect impatience has on the body.

Now I'm certain that you can find reasons why your impatience is manifesting. There's a lot to be impatient with. If you drive a car, work with children, are married, have in-laws, have parents, have neighbors, are alive ... you will be able to find "reasons" to be impatient. Pay **attention** to these "reasons" this week. You might just as easily call them "excuses" or those ever-popular "yeah, buts." Your job is to notice when they show up. What are they? When do they appear? What causes them? How good am I at staying centered in the world at hand? Pay **attention** and be fearless with what you are willing to know.

Directives for the Week: Continue with your morning journal and meditation.

When you wake up, make a special note of how you are feeling. Sometimes, we wake up anxious. What's that about? Occasionally, we wake up tired. Other times we wake up, bolt out of bed and are ready to meet the day. I love those days. Write about it.

Specifically, take time this week to focus your *attention* on being patient. Notice when you are making an effort to be patient and when it just happens naturally. Catch yourself in the act. Make a mental note – same goes for when you "lose it." What are the reasons/excuses for your impatience?

- At the end of each day, write out your "Mental Notes to Yourself" and expand on the event by asking yourself, "Why did I react that way?"

- That's all for this week other than to say, BE DILIGENT! Notice yourself ... and you will KNOW YOURSELF.

Patience Creates the Perfect Flow.

WEEK SIX

DAY TWO

Meditation: Relax • Release • Allow

During these next 10 or so minutes, let yourself relax by releasing anything that is causing you tension, anxiety or stress. Free yourself from the bondage of conditions that have no power other than the power you give them. You are "allowed" to step into your fullness, your pure potential, your personal destiny. Let yourself have that gift. Use the following reading to gently move you into a time of knowing:

> *I come to the silence to hear.*
> *I listen for the thoughts without words.*
> *A feeling creeps into my awareness.*
> *You are there in the feeling.*
> *I smile, I laugh, I cry, I know.*

Communication: In the past few days, how has patience been working for you? Do you find yourself to be a patient person? Are you as patient on the inside as you are perceived to be on the outside? Are you becoming aware of the "buttons" you possess? What are they? What makes you impatient?

In an earlier Boot Camp, it was shared that patience came easy to this particular gentleman. However, upon reflection, he realized that his patience was the result of apathy. He'd been disappointed so often, and with such disturbing results, that he'd stopped trying. He'd given up on many of his dreams and was settling for just "getting by." But to those who met him he was perceived as a patient man.

I found his sharing very perceptive. He didn't like patience week because he wanted to get rid of his patience and go out there and knock down walls. What he realized was that he wanted to get rid of his apathy and step back into his personal "Circle of Energy."

- What's your story surrounding patience? How have the last few days differed for you in relation to your level of patience and impatience?

- What sort of things are you feeling when you wake up in the morning? How do you perceive yourself?

- On a scale of one to 10, where do you land on the PATIENCE scale? How does that number feel to you?

- Write it in your journal and expand on it with each new day and awareness.

- For group work, share your personal story. Are you patient? Are you sure? When are you impatient? Why? Keep mindful of your time allotment. No cross-talking.

Remember: There is no correct answer to any of these questions. There are only YOUR answers, and they are meant to inform you, not upset you. Don't allow yourself to second-guess yourself. The journey is perfect.

Intention: It has been said that patience is a state of endurance under difficult circumstances. It could mean persevering in the face of provocation without becoming annoyed or upset. However, it can also be a character trait, something we "are" as opposed to something we "do" or "have." In terms of spirituality, patience is something inherent within. We don't have to work for it, we have to surrender to it. When we remove ourselves from the conditions of our life and tune into the field of energy that is always present, patience comes as naturally as the morning sunrise.

As one Boot Camper wrote: "I practice patience when I take time out from the emotion of something and allow a sense of calm to run through the situation, providing clarity on the next step. It makes my negative energy 'spinners' and 'drama drones' CRAZY!"

Way too often we stop short of a goal because we are impatient. We give up our **intention** because we aren't willing to allow it to grow and evolve in its perfect time. As another Boot Camper put it, "I realize that I've missed a lot of wonderful experiences because of my impatience, and I choose to change that about myself."

Attention/Accountability:

1. Did you meditate and journal each morning?

2. Are you paying **attention** to yourself in terms of patience?

3. Did you write down your feelings first thing in the morning?

If not, why not?

Quotes from Boot Camp

"I just feel like people should know better! How can you be patient with these people?"

"I'm always running late and so I'm always frustrated. Hard to be patient when you're always running late."

"Patience has to have a line, you know, a line between being patient and BLOWING UP."

"I've noticed that impatience spreads pretty quickly."

"'I should do that' is one of my favorite expressions/excuses. I really have to stop 'shoulding' on myself so much."

"I am most impatient when I am waiting for things to evolve and show up in divine time."

"Instead of hurry up and wait, how about step it up and allow?"

"For me, patience isn't waiting. It's living in the moment. It's actually something tangible, for me."

Continue with this week's directives!

Perfect Timing is a Choice!

Do the work ... LIVE THE RESULTS!

WEEK SEVEN
LISTEN/RESOLVE

WEEK SEVEN

DAY ONE

**Meditation**: 10-minute minimum

Today, take a moment before you begin meditating to set the **_intention_** of listening. When you clearly set your **_intention_**, the Universe responds with action. **_Allow_** your mind to stay open. Listen, receive, and discover the patience inherent in the quiet of the soul.

> _"Before you speak, it is necessary for you to listen,_
> _for God speaks in the silence of the heart."_
> _Mother Teresa_

For the next 10 or so minutes, take the opportunity to just listen. Begin with the idea of patience, and bring that feeling into your meditation. Keep it simple, peaceful and loving. Be gentle with your thoughts, guiding them back to **_Patience._**

**Communication**: Spending a week, mindful of the level of patience in my life, has always led me to certain facts that I might not have discovered otherwise. For instance, it never occurred to me that I didn't have to have the answer to every question as it was posed in any given moment. Not having the answer did not mean that I was ill-prepared or stupid. Perhaps, I discovered, living the question for a while was the very answer I needed. I go back to my mantra, "I know nothing. Now what can I learn?" It really opens up the floodgates of potentiality.

As you made your way through the week, did you notice how many times you were challenged with situations that called on you to exhibit patience? One morning, one of our Boot Campers said that every week, when the **intention** was announced, he felt like it was a "calling all cars" for whatever directive that was given. Patience week meant that every opportunity for patience was on its way. Of course, this makes perfect sense. When we focus our attention on something, it energizes the very thing we're focused on. If we are focusing on patience and a peaceful experience, then we are expanding the energy in that area. If we are focused on fear and worry, giving energy to an apprehensive feeling, then we find ourselves attracting that into our lives. Take this Boot Camper, for instance:

"I was on the freeway, the 405, and I found myself
stuck between these two trucks. Me, in my little MG Midget,
boxed in on the freeway at rush hour. And then I remembered
*it was '****Patience Week****' and I thought, of course."*

What's gone on in your life this week? How many opportunities did you have to be patient? Were you able to succeed? If not, did you look behind the impatience and see what was causing it? Overall, how did it go?

Take a look at your notes from the week. Rate your days on a 1-to-10 scale for your ability to exhibit patience.

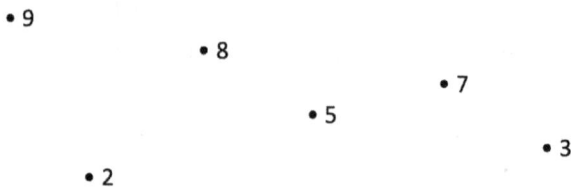

• 9

          • 8

                    • 7
            • 5

                      • 3

      • 2

Now connect the dots with a line. How crazy a roller coaster is your "patience" level?

The object here is to create a balanced life. To the degree that you have control over your mind, your thoughts, your beliefs, to that degree will you have control over your life. Patience, like everything else, is a choice! We are always at choice. We just aren't always patient. Just look at the line you drew, and you'll see the ride you're on. If you don't like the ride, don't buy the ticket. Buy a different one.

- If you are in a group, do this exercise together. Discuss the "ride" you're taking and how much control you have over it. Keep mindful of your time allotment. No cross-talking. Be patient with one another.

Intention: This week's Intention is ***Listen/Resolve.***

I listen for the sound of my Authentic Voice!

There are two parts to this week's Intention.

Part One: ***Listen***

The world is a very loud place – lots to hear and many voices crowding the airwaves. Everywhere we turn, we are assaulted by *noise*. The art of listening has become quite uncommon. Most often, in the midst of a conversation, I can actually see the person I'm speaking to not listening to what I'm saying in anticipation of what he or she plans to say. I certainly catch myself in that trap as well. People today speak over one another as though it were the only way to converse. Our contemporary playwrights are geniuses at capturing the way we talk without listening, interrupt without apology and communicate without thinking. We recognize it and laugh our heads off because it's so true.

Listening to what's outside our mind is one thing but listening to what's going on inside our mind and beyond, now that's another thing altogether. I believe that as we become more attuned to our authentic voice, we will be able to navigate the "surround sound" that is the world we live in, without becoming susceptible to its sometimes exhausting energy.

I hear based on where I'm at.

We all do. We hear what we want to hear, based on what we need to hear. Often, we hear based on our fears and our doubts. But are we listening, keeping our minds open and our thoughts free from experience? Are we able to listen as a child for the "new" thought, the new awareness, the new Truth? Are we able to distinguish the authentic from the plastic? I believe we can! If we hear based on where we're at, then we need to inform ourselves that we are in **heaven**, and we are ready to hear the angels sing. Why not? After all, "It is done unto us as we believe."

Part Two: ***Resolve everything in the moment.***

One of the reasons we have such a hard time listening for the "new" is because we're so clogged up with the "old." Every time we procrastinate and put something off until tomorrow, we're taking up precious space in our mind with something that we have labeled **TO DO.** These things become like little sinkers on the end of a fishing line. If you put too many on the line, it'll eventually snap. You won't be catchin' anything in that ocean.

Why resolve everything in the moment? Because you can – because you have the ability – and because you have the choice. A very funny writer in our Boot Camp stated one morning that her mother was like "General Patton." "My whole childhood was regimented. We did everything we were told and completed it like we were vying for medals. I think one year she actually did give out medals." She shared later that she realizes now that she stopped doing certain things as a reaction to her mother. Procrastination was her way of getting back at someone who wasn't even alive anymore.

Leaving things unresolved is like having a backed-up sink and not taking care of it. Eventually, you have to unclog it. The longer you wait, the more disgusting the contents. If you deal with each item as it goes down the drain, it goes down a lot easier.

Attention/Accountability: Pay **attention** this week to what you are hearing. Listen to the sounds of the world around you. Listen at home, at the office, in the market, at the bank. Listen to what the world is saying. Listen also for your reaction to what you are hearing. Listen within.

In your daily meditation, shut off the noise, the sounds and the chatter of your own thoughts. Listen intently for the Authentic Self. It may be a thought. It might be a feeling. It might be a color. Whatever it is, **_allow_** yourself to experience it. Enter the silence, listen, and see what comes next.

Pay special attention to things you put off "until tomorrow." Procrastination is a way of life for some people. They are always behind, clogged up, and crammed with things "to do." There never seems to be enough time and, therefore, it makes sense to put things on the back burner.

And yet, if we just take the time to resolve things in the moment, there will be far less to attend to on that fretful "tomorrow." In fact, there will be more time to do the things we want to do. And THAT is a beautiful thing!

Directives for the Week: Continue with your morning journal and meditation.

1. *Listen/Hear/Allow* – Meditate each morning following your journaling, for a minimum of 10 minutes. Your only objective is to **_Listen_**.

2. During the day, make a conscious effort to Listen to what is being said. Listen to what you are saying, to what is being said to you. Most importantly, listen to what is being said *within*.

3. At the end of each day, write "Today I Listen" on an index card

(or whatever works for you) and place it where you will see it upon awakening.

4. Resolve everything in the moment. Do not allow anything to go unresolved, no matter how insignificant it may appear. Make an immediate response to everything that comes up. If you find yourself not resolving things in the moment, figure out why.

Do it NOW!

__Meditation__: Listen

> *I have discovered a secret place within,*
> *where the thought goes into a mountain high above the din of the world.*
> *I have found in this mountain a place of peace and rest,*
> *A place of joy and comfort to the heart.*
> *I have found that the Secret Place of God is within my own Soul.*
> *I will listen for Thy Voice.*

Take a moment and listen to the world around you. Check in with what you are feeling in this very instant. How do you feel? How is it connected with what you are hearing? Now repeat the following:

> *I listen to the sound of my Authentic Voice.*

Repeat this a number of times until it drifts into the subconscious and frees your mind of the day's distractions. Drop into the quiet and while there, just listen.

__Communication__: What do you hear when you listen? Are you able to enter the quiet and hear? How is the world around you responding to you, now that you are listening to it?

What was it like to wake to the reminder, "Today I Listen?" Did you do it? If not, why? When you came across your reminder throughout the day, did it shift the experience in that moment? Were you able to listen to what you were saying, what was being said to you and to that voice within? Are you hearing more now that you are listening?

Are you a procrastinator? Now that you are focusing on resolving things in the moment, are you noticing your patterns? Are you able to respond to each situation with a resolute attitude? When we allow things to go unresolved, it's often because we somehow think we can't or don't have the capacity to resolve them. Sometimes we just won't because we resent General Patton.

- Use this opportunity to write your thoughts about this week thus far. As you write, listen to what you are thinking.

- For group work, share your personal story and keep notes on what you hear yourself thinking. Keep mindful of your time allotment. No cross-talking.

Intention: One of the great gifts of listening is that we begin to hear what was there all along. Shakespeare wrote, "If music be the food of love, play on." I like to think of music as anything that sings in our ears, like the sounds of trees swaying in the breeze, the crickets on a summer night or the waves crashing on a sandy beach. So much of what we hear these days feels like interruptive "noise" and yet, if we focus our minds on hearing beyond the sounds, we will be able to hear the beauty in every situation. It just takes one person to listen and then respond from an authentic "feeling" for the world to shift.

Years ago, I saw a video of a person in a subway listening to the music being piped onto the platform. He started swaying to the music. People passed him and ignored him at first, but then one by one they started to join him. Within a few moments, everyone was swaying to the music, and it looked like a scene from a movie, but it wasn't. It was a group of people at rush hour waiting for their commute to continue but taking the time to stop and listen. It begs the question: How much are we missing by our inability or reluctance or just forgetfulness to listen?

It truly is time for us all to Listen UP. Take the art of listening to a higher level of participation. Step up your game.

Listen UP!

Attention/Accountability:

1. Did you write each morning?

2. Have you kept up with your meditation in the morning? This week make sure to just LISTEN.

3. Are you resolving things in the moment? If not, are you figuring out why? Getting to the root of the behavior, the core belief, is the key to changing it.

4. Did you write yourself the note, "Today I Listen?" Did you carry it with you and refer to it throughout the day?

5. Did you pay **attention** throughout the day to the following voices:

- Your Own Voice

- Others

- The Voice Within

I'm just going to know that you are doing it ALL.

A poem from Boot Camp

"Love rights the space,
I exist long into the void.
And out of the darkness a constant battery –
My own assault. A Waging war that never ends.
And I cry to be held, the answers to be given.
Tell me the truth, it SCREAMS – Tell me the Truth.
A breath - The truth - a soft whisper, the faint beat of my heart.
The breathing slows and from the silence,
A whisper pierces and resonates,
As a bolt of lightning against the black sky
... SSHHH ... I am Here. LISTEN."

Written by: Rob Arbogast
(Boot Camp, Fall '07)

Continue with this week's directives!

"SSHHH ... I am Here. LISTEN!"

Do the work ... LIVE THE RESULTS!

WEEK EIGHT
BOUNDARIES/PRIORITIES

WEEK EIGHT

DAY ONE

**Meditation**: 10-minute minimum

> _I do because I can. I can because I know._
> _I know because I Am._

As you continue to listen from within your meditation, allow your mind to know the truth, that you can accomplish whatever you decide to accomplish. Hear what comes up and resolve it in the moment. You can because you know you can. You know because YOU ARE the I AM!

**Communication**: Shared during Boot Camp:

"When I listen my whole world calms down."

"The world is a very loud place when you actually stop and listen to it. I need to stop more often, I think."

"Most of the noise I hear seems to be coming from my own head."

"Listening and resolving has transformed my work performance. I move into action and do the work task that is right in front of me instead of being distracted by hundreds of other things. Who knew?"

"Listening came in handy on a first date. The result is that I am having a second date tomorrow. No procrastination here."

"I feel like there's a committee in my head. They all talk at the same time. Nobody's listening."

One thing I recognize about my life is that I have become desensitized to the sounds around me. I walk by a Starbucks and see people with their earbuds working on their computers and I realize that we are all trying to create a space of our own in the midst of a very busy world. It's interesting that we now create space for ourselves in the "Cloud." Ever wonder where that "Cloud" is?

In the world of quantum, we are told that everything is made up of particles and space and that most of what we call life is just SPINNING SPACE, expanding, growing, evolving and creating. The question is, what are WE doing with this "Space?" And how much of it are we listening to?

Speaking of space, what are we doing with the space within our minds? How are we reacting to what we are hearing on the inside? What do we tell ourselves? Do we even take the time to hear what we think, or do we live reactionary lives that fly by at an alarming pace? It's a choice that we can resolve in this present moment. This past week has been designed to prove to you that you can resolve *anything* in the present moment. As one Boot Camper put it:

"The chatter in my head is the lack of decision. Decisions quiet my mind."

Resolving things in the moment frees up the next moment to the unexpected possibility of the new. This is what we are looking for, an opening to a higher conscious awareness. Listening to the silence, resolving in the moment, hearing the Authentic Self; all of this begins the journey to that opening within.

- Make a list of what you learned about yourself this week. Were you able to resolve things in the moment? Did you experience a new communication level as you listened more clearly?

- As you write, listen to what you are thinking. See if you can combine listening with expressing your thoughts. Ultimately that is our goal: to connect to Life in such a way as to allow it to inform us on every level.

- If you are in a group, share your experience with one another. Try to listen as others speak, without judgment or opinion. See what happens. Share it. (Keeping mindful of your time allotment). No cross-talking.

Intention: This week's Intention is ***Boundaries/Priorities.***

There are two parts to this week's Intention.

Part One: ***Boundaries***

There are many types of boundaries. Much like the witches in Oz, there are good boundaries and there are bad boundaries. The good ones are those that you set for specific reasons. The bad ones are those that go up as defense mechanisms for perceived "evil" and ones that were created by past experiences that we might not even be aware of. We call those "walls," and we spend much of our lives climbing over them or hitting them to the point of exhaustion.

Our ***intention*** this week is to identify our boundaries and tag them as either useful or damaging. Once we do that, we can then go about the business of obliterating the walls and opening the horizons to a brighter day. We might even get to meet the Wizard, and eventually realize that we had the answer all along.

> *"Self-image sets the boundaries of individual accomplishment"*
> *Maxwell Maltz*

One of the most powerful boundaries is our estimation of ourselves, our self-image. We come up against our own walls of limitation every time we identify ourselves as anything other than pure, infinite potentiality. Within each of us is the spark of creative genius. It's not something we have to acquire; we already have it. In fact, we already ARE IT.

Part Two: *Priorities*

How do you decide what to do? What makes one thing important to accomplish and another thing to put aside for later? Why do you do the things you do? It's important to know.

There are two reasons for doing things: obligation and passion. Occasionally, we do things because we have nothing else to do and that falls in line with not really doing but existing. We're talking here about things you "decide" to do.

Are you doing them because you feel you "have to?" Or are you doing them because you are passionate about yourself? Mother Teresa once said that fulfilling one's purpose in life is to find one's passion and live it. Are you doing that?

Attention/Accountability: Pay attention this week to the boundaries that exist in your life. See where you have created them for a reason and where they seem to have appeared out of nowhere. Does this boundary meet your needs or is it keeping you from them? Is it a good boundary or a bad boundary?

Also, pay *attention* to your priorities. What is it that moves something to the top of your list? What allows others to go unresolved? How does procrastination play out in the face of priorities?

Directives for the Week: Continue with your morning journal and meditation.

1. Each morning when you wake up, make a list of your priorities for the day. Jot down how they make you feel.

2. Before you go to sleep each night, go over your list of priorities from the morning. Did you succeed at meeting them, or did they get pushed aside for other, more immediate priorities? Note how this played out in your day.

3. Keep an ongoing list of boundaries as you continue through the week. Next to each one, write either GOOD or BAD. You can also write down PENDING if you aren't sure.

Boundaries and priorities are directly linked to your self-worth. When we love ourselves, respect ourselves and insist on only that which will feed our souls and nourish our minds, we prioritize and set boundaries that reflect a healthy understanding of who we are.

"There is Good for me and I ought to have it!"
Emma Curtis Hopkins

WEEK EIGHT

DAY TWO

Meditation: Boundaries/Priorities

My mind stays open to a field of infinite possibility.
Air is plenty, sky is limitless, light is ever present.
I see, I feel, I smell, I touch, and yet I never move.
I AM movement. I AM sky. I AM touch.
My walls have no purpose.
My boundaries have no reason.
The only thing to do ... is TO BE!

Communication: I've heard it said that boundaries are signposts of how far we are willing to go in any situation. It is also how far we are willing to let someone in. Is it safe to be an open door for anyone to enter? How open are you to hearing what others have to say? How well do you take criticism? Are you conscious of other people's boundaries?

Where are your walls? Are you closed in by your own inability to go beyond your comfort zone? What is your comfort zone? Is it something that feeds you, or holds you back? How comfortable do you need to be? Where's the line? Where's the boundary?

Are you your No. 1 priority? When you made your list of priorities for the day, were you on that list? What position were you in?

- As you ponder the answers to these questions, notice how you feel. Jot down your feelings in your journal.

- Make a list of your current priorities and number them in terms of importance. When you are done, see if the number of times you focus on each of these priorities matches up with their placement of importance.

- List your top three priorities. Now put them in order. What was your No. 1 priority? Are you doing all you can to fulfill and support that priority? If not, there's a strong possibility that it's not your number ONE priority.

- For group work, share your personal story. Do the exercise regarding the priorities and read them to the group, commenting on how they match up with your level of attention to each priority. (Keeping mindful of your time allotment). No cross-talking.

Intention: In a world where you know that you can do it all, in what order will you do it? That's the question. As one Boot Camper put it, "sometimes there is so much to do that I get overwhelmed and do nothing." Prioritizing is about "choice," focusing on one thing at a time and giving it our full **attention.**

Passion versus obligation in priorities is quite eye opening.

Our goal is to create a life where we live from the inside out. We want, once and for all, to live a meaningful existence. We look to recognize our passions, our desires, our deepest aspirations; and we allow them to inform our actions. We break down the walls, the excuses, the limitations, and we move into the realization that we must become our first priority. Ask yourself, what stops you from putting yourself first? Whatever that is, it's time to free yourself from its grip.

Attention/Accountability:

1. Did you wake up to your priorities and make a list of what the day had in store?

2. Have you kept up with your meditation, building it into a rich Spiritual Practice?

3. Throughout the day, did you consciously acknowledge your boundaries, naming them good, bad or pending?

4. At night, did you check your priority list to see how you did? Did you do what you needed to do about what you said was your No. 1 priority? Remember, there is no limit to what you can do.

"There is good in the world, and I ought to have it!"
Emma Curtis Hopkins

To have it ... you have to take it!

Quotes from Boot Camp

"This week I saw for the first time that I wasn't my number one priority. I put everyone else before me."

"I don't trust myself to choose wisely, so the walls go up."

"I've learned that 'no' is a complete sentence when needing to remove myself from yet another enabling or co-dependent experience."

"This thing called 'other people' forces my hand to create boundaries."

"Talk about crossing boundaries, my mother ought to have a company called . She thinks it's okay to fix me up with whomever she wants. I need to set that boundary and I'll call it GOOD!"

"My priorities aren't the same from day to day, especially now."

"Boundaries are the maze; priorities are the cheese. I guess I am the rat."

Continue with this week's directives!

We can do it all! The question is, in what order?

Do the work ... LIVE THE RESULTS!

WEEK NINE
LIFE FORCE

WEEK NINE

DAY ONE

THE HALFWAY POINT

Congratulations, you have made it to the halfway point of Spiritual Boot Camp. If you've stuck to the program, you are much more aware of what is going on inside your mind and you should be seeing changes reflected in the way your life is unfolding. They say knowledge is power – well, Self-knowledge is Self-power.

Now, it's time to recommit to the program and, by doing so, recommitting to *Yourself*. Begin your meditation today with the following:

*Meditation***:** During the second half of Spiritual Boot Camp, increase your time in meditation. Going forward, it is a given that you will spend no fewer than 10 minutes, but preferably more.

> *I rise to a higher consciousness.*
> *I step into my Individual Power!*

Repeat this at least three times. Allow yourself to hear the words as they are formed in your mouth. Listen as your "Voice" repeats the Truth of who and what you are capable of being and doing. You can and do "rise" above every situation into a higher consciousness of Truth. You ARE the Power.

Communication: Following your meditation, take a moment to think about **YOUR WORD.** How does it feel, eight weeks later? Is it applicable to what you've learned about yourself? In terms of priorities, has Your Word become an important part of your day-to-day life? Are **You** your No. 1 priority?

"Action expresses priorities."
Mahatma Gandhi

Talk is cheap, and it's getting cheaper by the year. It's all too easy to say what you are going to do. Everyone has a plan, a dream, a tomorrow they will tell you about. But until they can show you, it's all just feathers in the wind. If you have a priority, and really make it important, you will back it up with ***Action***.

I once heard an acting teacher say to someone, "If you were arrested for being an actor, would there be enough evidence to convict you? Or would you get off because they could only pin you with being a waiter?" Point made, at least it was to that guy. Without naming names, he's a very successful movie actor today.

> *Very often we let a relationship become a priority,*
> *but without making ourselves first,*
> *there isn't a foundation for the relationship.*

This came up from a workshop where a woman was expressing how, throughout a 26-year marriage, she allowed herself to be swallowed up by the needs of everyone else around her. The No. 1 priority was always someone else's need. Getting back to her own needs prompted her to step out on her own and rekindle the relationship with herself. Within a year, her marriage was back on track. Not only that, it was more passionate and vibrant than ever. The relationship wasn't the problem, her priorities were.

"When I don't make myself the number one priority, I lose my freedom."
Oprah Winfrey

Are you your No. 1 priority? Look at your lists from throughout the week. What are they telling you about your commitment level to your proclaimed priorities? What do you need to know here? Does something need to change? Write out a new priority list addressing these insights. Remember, a priority list is not a To Do List. For instance, you could make fun of your No. 1 priority. Your health could be your No. 1 priority and would involve making decisions on all fronts that support your healthful living. Or maybe it's just conscious living, the priority to stay awake, no matter what.

On the boundaries front, how would you feel if you were to drop all of your boundaries? Would you feel vulnerable or excited for the future? Do you hear a voice in your head screaming I NEED MY BOUNDARIES? Well, you very well might. But the goal is to get to that place where you are a limitless landscape with no boundaries, walls or borders. Once we step into our own authority with absolute certainty, there will be no need for boundaries or walls of any kind. We will only attract those things into our experience that resonate with our True Nature. Our world will be filled with the power of "yes" and the power of "no" (and there is great power in the word "no.") You will know exactly what to say, when to say it, and how to live from your own choices.

"All good things must come to an end." This came up for one Boot Camper who realized that the belief in all good things coming to an end was a wall that needed to be torn down. She replaced that wall with "all good things lead to even greater things." Boundary eliminated, landscape infinite.

> One of the most destructive boundaries we have
> is our relationship to money.

We create walls of resistance in the abundant flow of money. On one side, we hold tight to what we have, worrying that there won't be enough. On the other side, we struggle to claim what's ours, working overtime to build a fortress and amass a wealth that quite often don't make us happy to begin with.

"I just don't understand how I can be okay for such a long stretch of time and then all of a sudden I'm back in struggle mode." This was shared one night online during a session. Everyone chimed in with his or her own struggles concerning money.

Given that it was Boundary Week, it was handled by recognizing the wall of fear that surrounds money. When we tear down the fear and step into the certainty that comes with knowing who we are, money does not and cannot become an issue. **Money isn't the issue**. The core belief of fear is the issue.

- Before we move on to this week's *Intention*, take a moment here to write out any and all boundaries/walls/beliefs that you may recognize concerning your relationship to money and the negative effect they may be having on your manifesting the life you want. Once you put them on paper, leave them there. Replace them with beliefs that will enhance your circle of energy and launch a new era of prosperity and financial freedom.

If you are in a group, share your feelings on these topics. (Keeping mindful of your time allotment). No cross-talking.

Intention: This week's Intention is *Life Force.*

> *"Kid, I've flown from one side of this galaxy to the other, and I've seen a lot of strange stuff, but I've never seen 'anything' to make me believe that there's one all-powerful Force controlling everything."*
> *Han Solo to Luke Skywalker*

Years ago, revisiting **Star Wars** with my eight-year-old son was an awesome experience. When I saw the movies the first time, I wasn't so in tune with metaphysics and New Thought. Watching them years later, I was blown away by how much Truth there is in the story. And I love that they use Han Solo to play the role of the reluctant hero. He wants proof, and the movie uses that opportunity to show him the proof.

There is a Life Force back of everything. It's not a separate entity predetermining our destiny, but an energy that moves through us and is there for us to use. It intuits through our mind and allows us to create based on our thoughts.

"Change your thinking, change your life."
Ernest Holmes

Depending on what thoughts we put into our mind, how we believe and what we believe, our world manifests proportionately. If I think (believe) success, I am successful. If I think (believe) love, I will experience love. If, conversely, I think (believe) lack – well, I just don't. I know how that movie ends. And thus, our Life Force, flowing through us, ***allows*** us to be creators of our own creations. Sometimes we're riding high and other times we're hitting bottom. It's an eternal roller coaster, and yet it doesn't have to be. It's the same Life Force, whether we use it to create happiness or despair.

If we are aware enough to notice, we will always know which things create a flow of Life Force and which ones suck it out of us. For example: judgment, fear, stress, arguments, they all deplete the Life Force flow. Notice I said 'flow.' Your Life Force can never be depleted. You can put a kink in the hose and temporarily stop the flow, but you can never erase the Source.

The question this week will be, do you know what makes you happy? Do you know what things energize you, make you sing and dance and get giddy? Do you know what calms you, soothes you, relaxes your mind and eases your body? Do you know yourself? The answer is, yes. Within you is an intuitive energy that is always seeking to experience itself. It's that voice that tells you to go for a walk in the park, take a swim, or just close your eyes and breathe into the Truth. We know more than we give ourselves credit for knowing. This week we get to put our conscious ***attention*** on the Life Force behind all things. It just so happens to be contained within each of us.

Attention/Accountability: Pay **attention** this week to what makes your heart sing and what gets stuck in your throat. Notice what fills you up and what leaves you empty. **Allow** yourself to be brutally honest with respect to what really brings you happiness and what doesn't.

If you find yourself judging things you are doing or getting stressed out about those things that deplete your energy, stop and reframe. Just pay Attention to how it all makes you feel. Remember, you are always just a choice away from changing it. Don't get stuck in the past, use the present to tap into that Life Force. Notice how you can ... and then DO.

Directives for the Week: Continue with your morning journal and meditation.

1. Make a list of the areas in your life where you are being fed and nourished. Then write down those things that take away your Life Force. Do this impersonally and with respect for your past choices. Do this daily, refining the list as the week progresses.

2. Do one thing each day that activates your Life Force. Try to find new and different things that will accomplish this task. If you usually cannot find the time to take a nap during a busy day, make room for one. If you've been longing for that massage appointment but don't feel you can afford it, make an exception. Take a walk before you go to bed, look at the stars, smell the jasmine. And in a pinch just tell yourself something about you that is remarkable. Don't let a day go by without activating your Life Force.

> *"May the Force be with you!"*
> *Obi-Wan Kenobi*

WEEK NINE

DAY TWO

__Meditation__: Have you expanded your meditation beyond the 10 minutes? If not, give it a thought.

Today, as you meditate, ***allow*** your mind to feel the flow of energy in your body. Feel and hear the pulse and rhythm of your blood as it travels in perfect time through your body. Feel yourself living inside your skin. Feel the chair you are sitting in, or the air around you if you are standing. Become one with everything around you and then begin to feel the Universal Life Force that supports and holds you in its rhythm and song.

"Music and rhythm find their way into the secret places of the soul"
Plato

Communication: It is very clear to me that, when I take action in my life, when I make a strong decision to do something active, my Life Force starts to swell. As I move, so does the energy that is my soul. Passion is one way to measure Life Force. If you are passionate about what you are doing, you will always be increasing your Life Force. And you can feel when that happens.

I remember when I was opening in a new musical in Philadelphia. As the title character, I was to open the show by coming onstage alone and singing the first notes of the play acapella (without accompaniment). The musical note was given to me as I approached the stage and I was required to hold onto it until my cue to enter. Well, it was opening night and for some reason, once I got in place, we had to hold for 10 minutes.

Somewhere around minute seven, I lost the note. I could feel the energy in my body start to swell. Of course, this was fear, combined with excitement and uncertainty of the outcome. Just as I was about to go off and get the note, the cue light went on and I was caught. I walked onstage with my little lantern (I was playing a young Irish coal miner) and I began to sing. I looked out into the audience and realized how incredibly happy I was to be doing what I was doing. I completely forgot about the note, or whether or not I was in the right key. My Life Force came from behind and drove me right from that starting moment clear through to curtain call. Passion prevails! (I was about a half step above the note and I slipped down once the orchestra came in. No one noticed, or so they said.)

- In the past few days, have you noticed when you are energized and when you feel low? More importantly, have you made special note of what it is that causes you to feel one way or the other?

- When you actively decide to do something to increase your Life Force, what happens?

- Write in your journal your experience of doing something each day to increase your Life Force. How does it feel? Are you doing it? Does it come naturally, or do you have to force it? What would it be like to do this for the rest of your life? What would change?

- For group work, share your personal story with one another. Pay close attention to the Life Force in the room. What causes it to shift? What propels you and what causes you to tune out? (Keeping mindful of your time allotment). No cross-talking.

Intention: One Boot Camper shared that when she put together her list of things that fed her soul and the list of things that "zapped" her, it was surprising how the "zap" list was so much longer. She realized how much more attention she put on things in her life that drained her energy. She then sat down and wrote out all the things she loved to do and consciously increased the side of the equation that fed her Life Force. By the time she was done, her "soul" list included chocolate fudge cake with vanilla bean and chocolate chip mint ice cream. With that in the mix, who can remember what "zaps" them?

On the heels of Priority Week, it would be wise to make our priority courting those things that feed our Life Force.

Attention/Accountability:

1. Did you write each morning and evening, going over your discoveries and refining them as you went along?

2. Have you kept up with your meditation in the morning, extending your time to what feels good?

3. Have you made time to do something each day that activates your Life Force?

If not, make sure you know the reason you didn't do the work. When we can't take the time to enhance our own lives with things we love to do, or if we can't come up with a list of things we love to do, there's clearly some core belief, some B.S. holding you back.

Quotes from Boot Camp

"Never force the Force!"

"Micromanaging every little thing about my life is exhausting. And it eats into my Life Force."

"Being nice to myself isn't easy. Why is that? That is the question."

"I feel like I'm having spiritual contractions giving birth to this Life Force."

"Sometimes what I might consider 'no big deal' really is something that is either activating or zapping my Life Force."

"This week I took a belly dancing class to feed my Life Force. I've never laughed so hard in all my life. Whatever it takes, right?

Continue with this week's directives!

Your purpose is your passion. Don't go looking for it. It will find you!

Do the work ... LIVE THE RESULTS!

WEEK TEN
PERFECTIONISM

__Meditation__: Expanding beyond 10 minutes. What are you up to now?

> *"There is a vitality, a life force, an energy,*
> *a quickening that is translated through you into action,*
> *and because there is only one of you in all of time,*
> *this expression is unique. ...*
> *It is not your business to determine how good it is,*
> *nor ... how it compares with other expressions.*
> *It is your business to keep it yours clearly and directly,*
> *to keep the channel open."*
> *Martha Graham to Agnes DeMille*

The great dancer and choreographer Martha Graham was a conduit for creativity. She intuited the spark of individuality and allowed it to flow through her in the form of brilliant, imaginative movement. She frequently spoke of a Life Force present in all, and she taught her students to "become the vessel, the channel for this life force to express."

Reread the quote above and allow it to take you to a place where you *__allow__* yourself to be the "vessel." Quiet all thought and chatter, and just hear the words of Martha Graham as you step into the silence of your mind. Continue to bring forth her words if you find yourself drifting into the world of facts and details.

__Communication__: In researching the many definitions of Life Force, I was most intrigued by the following: "The vital principle or animating force within all living things." In Quantum Physics it is better known as an energetic field of space and particles. It is sometimes referred to as a Life Principle. And while modern quantum physicists are becoming more and more vocal about an infinite world of "energy" animating all life, it is still considered hypothesis and not law.

Still, we know that what we put our **attention** on expands. There is a definite reaction when something is being observed. This is called "The Observer Effect." When we take our individual Life Force and concentrate it in any one area, we are expanding the energy from within.

- Did you take the time this week to focus your energy on your Life Force? Did you do something every day to enhance your circle of energy? What did it feel like?

- Were you surprised by the lists of things that deplete your energy? Are you willing to eliminate them from your life? Willingness is the first step.

- Have you continued with your meditation and journaling?

One of the greatest tools in developing Mental Muscle is the commitment to Spiritual Practice. One of our Boot Campers wrote: "I've taken countless workshops, seminars, classes, read spiritual books, lived in Osho's commune and STILL I slide back to square one." What we realized was that each of these things were attempts to accumulate spirituality, not tap into what is already here. Spiritual Practice is tapping into the Life Force that we all have and **allowing** it to take us on Its journey. Sporadic attempts at "becoming" spiritual will almost always fail in the face of worldly conditions. What we need is a Spiritual Practice that works for us in our own unique, personal way.

"Just going to church once a week doesn't make you spiritual any more than living in your garage makes you a car."
Anonymous

What really makes you sing? What raises those goose bumps from under your skin to mountains of tingling flesh? Do you remember your first concert? Mine was a John Denver concert in Philadelphia. When he started singing "Thank God I'm a Country Boy," I thought my body was going to explode. And I lived in a row home in a suburb of Philadelphia. But that didn't matter. There was just something about that moment in time. What was it for you? And more importantly, what IS IT NOW?

- Go over your list of things that feed your soul and see if you can "enhance" it with some things you've only dreamed of. Write them down and then DO THEM!

Intention: This week's Intention is **_Perfectionism._**

> *"They say that nobody is perfect.*
> *Then they tell you practice makes perfect.*
> *I wish they'd make up their minds."*
> *Wilt Chamberlain*

I love this quote. We live in a world that can be very confusing at times – if we let it. I grew up being told to continually work on becoming perfect at something. It didn't matter what it was, just find something you're good at and perfect it. So, I tried playing the guitar. I was good, not perfect. I played the piano. I was okay, not even good. I sang. I could see perfection at times, but at others, I would miss the mark. Broadway, Hollywood, London, musicals, movies, record deals, all opportunities to show that I was No. 1, and perfect. Each one was a lesson in missing the mark. So close, so often and, by others' standards, succeeding so brilliantly. But perfect? No! And it was never good enough for me.

I was always too interested in what "they" had to say. As if there was a committee somewhere who had their perfect idea of me in mind and I was supposed to measure up to what "they" decided was my perfect ten. So where do we get the idea of striving for perfection? It seems that the more you try to be perfect, the more you realize that it is an impossibility. For one thing, life is subjective. A perfect ten to one man could be a seven to another and then someone else comes along and calls it a three. So how do you even gauge what perfection is? It could drive you crazy spending a lifetime of trying to become perfect. And that's the problem. We are trying to **become** perfect when we already **are** perfect. How can you become what you already are? Good question!

> *"When you aim for perfection, you discover it's a moving target."*
> *George Fisher*

When Wilt Chamberlain writes, "I wish they'd make up their minds" it seems to me that he swishes it right through the net. (By the way, I was one of the "ball boys" for the Philadelphia 76ers when he played there.) We have to make up our minds that we already are perfect before we can actually tap into that perfection. We will never find it "out there." We do things **from** a place of perfection, not gain perfection from doing something well.

In changing your perspective about **perfection**, you will begin to step into an awareness of your True Potential far beyond anything you have experienced thus far. Instead of reaching for things, you will **allow** them to come to you.

> *Perfection! It's an **inside job**.*

And it's not about being No. 1. I was involved in a conversation where someone mentioned he had won a bronze medal at the Olympics in diving. We all just stopped for a moment to take in what we'd just heard. And then someone said, "what did it feel like to lose the gold?" I was shocked that this was the follow up. As though winning the bronze wasn't good enough. Being No. 3 in the world wasn't perfect? So close, but no cigar. And yet that's how we think sometimes.

Attention/Accountability: This week, pay attention to instances when you are **trying** to be perfect. Recognize your frustration when things aren't going the way you think they should be going. See everything in a new light. Notice when the "crazy" perfectionist rears its stressful head and when striving for perfection feels healthy and good. Make special note of when you feel "perfect" and when you feel "less than." What is happening to create the difference in perception?

Directives for the Week: Continue with your morning journal. Empty your mind of whatever thoughts you wish to release.

1. Upon waking, take a moment after your morning journaling to meditate on the **perfection** that is the coming day. "Expect" only good to show up, recognizing that the perfection in you attracts the perfection of the world around you.

2. At night, write about your day. Make a list of all the reasons you ARE perfect and all the proof you have that you are NOT perfect. Let yourself be fearless and don't judge what comes up. It's less important what you find and more important what you DO with what you find. Be creative.

Perfection begins and ends with the Truth!

*You are already **PERFECT!***

WEEK TEN

DAY TWO

Meditation: **The Quantum Universe is perfect!**

"Our mental attitude must be one of denial toward every false condition that opposes the principle of Life as one of absolute perfection."
Ernest Holmes

Bring into meditation the following affirmation:

My life is unfolding perfectly in this Perfect Universal Field of Love.

Communication: During one Boot Camp session, someone shared that they could find the perfection in themselves when they got quiet, and the world was quiet around them. The problem started when they came out of meditation and had to deal with "other people" who clearly weren't perfect. Ever have that feeling?

I reminded myself, in that moment, that it was never about "other people," but always about me. My job is to see the perfection in others as easily as I can see it in myself. If I'm seeing imperfection, I must be relating to something in myself that recognizes it. Now this isn't to say that I walk around like a lemming, following blindly the idea that there is *only* perfection in the world. I know that's not true on a human level. But I also know that what comes into my orbit is something for me to find the "good" in, something for me to "know."

Then someone else stated that she could always find the perfection in "others" but could never find it in herself. She talked about spending her whole life trying to be perfect, only to weigh in at "barely acceptable."

Again, trying to be perfect is a hopeless crusade.

- How often in the past few days did you find yourself striving for perfection? Do others, who seem to miss the mark, frustrate you? How does that affect you and your quest for inner peace?

- Can you find glimpses of your perfection in your meditation? Are you able to stay there and activate that energy into your daily living?

- What does your list look like? What proof do you have that you ARE perfect? And what did you find that proved your IMPERFECTION?

- Take a moment and reflect on these questions. Note your feelings in your journal for future reference.

- For group work, share your thoughts and your lists with one another. (Keeping mindful of your time allotment). No cross-talking.

Intention: Perfection is: "the quality or state of being perfect, a freedom from fault or defect, a flawlessness," and my personal favorite: "a maturity." There is a deep wisdom within all of us that is as mature as the Universe is old. When we come to understand that all of us are, indeed, perfect in our own unique ways, we reach an "understanding that surpasseth all understanding." Suddenly that dent in the front fender represents a journey, not a mistake. A failed marriage becomes a relationship that ran its course and was perfect for what it was. An expected job offer that never comes represents an opportunity for something even better. Perfection is what we ARE, not what we DO.

Perfection, if we ***allow*** it, will call to us. The calling will spring us into action and we will find ourselves soaring through our lives with passion and pizzazz (yes, I really said pizzazz).

Attention/Accountability:

1. Did you start each day with the expectation of perfection, taking that consciousness into your meditation?

2. Did you pay **attention** throughout the day to your perfectionism and look at what's behind the behavior?

3. Did you write about your day each night, adding to your lists of proof on both sides of the perfection equation?

4. Are you paying attention to moments of perfectionism creeping into your Life Force?

If you are doing the work, you'll recognize the benefits.

Quotes from Boot Camp

"Trying to be perfect leads to paralysis."

"I already am perfect? Joke's on me then. I guess once I realize I already am perfect, it'll give a whole new meaning to perfectionism."

"What I am realizing is that my apparent lack of perfection is based on my perception of what OTHER people think of as perfect."

"So, if I already am perfect, why do I work so hard to prove it?"

"Am I a perfectionist? Trying to get the question answered perfectly was the answer in and of itself."

Continue with this week's directives!

Don't look outside to prove your perfection!

Do the work ... LIVE THE RESULTS!

WEEK ELEVEN
INTENTION

WEEK ELEVEN

DAY ONE

**Meditation**: A Growing Experience

"Every particular in nature, a leaf, a drop, a crystal, a moment of time is related to the whole, and partakes of the perfection of the whole."
Ralph Waldo Emerson

As you meditate today, give yourself permission to disappear into the wholeness of the Universe. Take your attention off your physical self and put it on the world around you, above you, below you, beyond the stars and planets to that place of infinite expanse.

Feel your Oneness with everything and experience what "Perfection" feels like from within its presence.

**Communication**: By this point in the program, you have been asking yourself a lot of questions. You have purposefully been giving specific attention to things about yourself that are personal and revealing. Some of these things are merely facts that can be changed in the presence of a new belief, a better decision. Others are Truths that are irrefutable. A lot of it could be used to prove your imperfection; and some of it could uphold your position as innately perfect.

The Spiritual Truth that perfection lies within, and that we are that perfection to the degree that we **accept** this Truth, is a motivating force behind Spiritual "enlightenment." When you know this about yourself, there is no limit to what you can accomplish.

"Know thyself!"
Socrates

In today's world, we know ourselves based on so many things, most of which are transient. Who I was yesterday may be completely obliterated by what I know today and how I react given certain facts that are revealed to me. All of it shifts and all of it changes.

One Boot Camper noticed that during Perfection Week she was so up and down that she started talking to herself out loud. "What's the matter with you? Yesterday you said you were perfect. Were you lying?" It feels like that sometimes, doesn't it? One day, we recognize our greatness and then something happens that makes us feel less than perfect. When I was an actor, I remember reading reviews that bounced back and forth between praise and criticism. And the funny thing was that I always remembered the criticism more vividly than the praise.

The One perfect, changeless Truth in all of this is Life Itself. There's an Ernest Holmes quote: "*Perfect God, Perfect Human, Perfect Being,*" that has always resonated with me. (Actually, he wrote "Perfect Man; but I've taken the liberty of bringing the lingo of Holmes' generation into the 21st Century.) However you understand God, and even if you don't believe in a God, I believe we're beginning to realize the perfection of the Universe and the ability of Life to unfold perfectly. For me, I've taken Ernest Holmes' quote and reimagined it to be: "Perfect Life, Perfect Human, Perfect Human BEING Perfect Life." The **being** part of that equation, for me, is a verb, not a noun – *being* Perfect Human, representing Perfect Life.

How about seeing the perfection in others? Is that a challenge? I remember in our very first Boot Camp when I announced that it was Perfection Week. One of our gang was a stand-up comic and said, "Shut the door and close the windows it's gonna be a long week." He was referring to all the "crazy" he experienced in his line of work and how he could find perfection within himself to some degree, but finding it in others was a real chore. I told him, as I have told myself on numerous occasions, "... if you can't find perfection in others, you won't find it in yourself ... and vice versa."

- How are you living this understanding of perfection? How does it show up in your life? What does it look like? Do you naturally gravitate to knowing that it's all perfect, or do you need it to prove itself for you to see it? Are you letting perfection call to you – or are you calling to it?

- How did your week change with the expectation that it was guided by the perfection of the Universe unfolding perfectly? Did knowing that you already are perfect change your reactions to things throughout your day?

- Did you find that, at the end of your day, you were able to notice a shift in perception? How well did you do holding back from human perfectionism, both with yourself and with others? Look back over what you wrote. Do you get it now?

*You already **ARE** perfect!*

- If you are in a group, share your thoughts with one another. How does the consciousness of the room shift with each share? Keep mindful of your time allotment No cross-talking.

Intention: This week we focus on **_Intention_** itself.

"Our intention creates our reality."
Wayne Dyer

Now that you know that you come from perfection, what are you going to do about it? Knowing something doesn't mean that you are living from that point of view. We have spent the past 10 weeks focusing on Intentions. They have been specific to each week but, nonetheless, they have been directed toward a result. That result is an awareness of the Self, the higher Self.

The word intention means to act with purpose, to have a definite goal or destination in mind. It is the larger decision to create something in our lives. An intention to do, or to be or to have, sets the gears in motion for it to become a reality.

An intention is not a plan! It's what's behind the plan.

Is it your intention to succeed? Is it your intention to struggle? Is it your intention to **allow** things to just happen? Intention is a first cousin to expectancy, and yet it has its own set of distinctions. I remember once sitting in class with my teacher, Dr. David Walker, and hearing him say, "You know you have an intention if you actually DO IT! I can say I'm going to the movies but unless I look up the schedule, get in the car, drive to the theatre, buy the ticket (and popcorn) and climb into my seat, I can't really say I intended to go to the movies. If I don't do it, I never intended it. I just **thought** about doing it."

*Intentions are **thoughts activated**!*

So, intentions are thoughts activated. Perhaps, given the previous scenario, I could have started out for the movies, noticed a breathtaking sunset on the horizon and ended up at the beach. Did I intend to go to the movies? Yes! It was just that a new intention came into play and then I followed through with that intention. Anything wrong with that? Depends on the movie, the sunset and the individual involved. If you were meeting someone at the movie, you might have thought twice about shifting gears. Still, both intentions were put into play. They were both **activated.**

I bring up this last scenario because it came up in one of our Boot Camps. If intentions are thoughts activated, and we shift gears, did we ever have the first intention strongly enough to follow through with it? My answer to that is, don't drive yourself crazy. I believe that if I act on my intentions and stay open to the Life Force within, knowing that I fully expect my life to play out for my highest Good, then I will always know what to do, when to do it and who to do it with.

Unless you marry intention to action,
you end up with only a brief affair.

I will always remember my Grandmother Mellon saying to my older brother, "If you intend to do it, then just do it, don't tell me about it." It was one of her catch phrases. My brother was always saying what he was going to do but rarely ever did it. I, on the other hand, never told anyone what I was going to do ... I just did it. That way, no one had the chance to talk me out of it. I still do that today. I keep my intentions close to the vest. I always tell my students that sharing your intentions with everyone is a sure-fire way to talk yourself out of something. Find someone you trust and share it with that person if you need to talk it through. Otherwise, state your intention to yourself and then DO IT. Otherwise, it's not an intention.

If you intend to do it, then just do it!

Attention/Accountability: Pay **attention** this week to your declared intentions. Are you acting on them, or are they just thoughts? Get clear on the difference between the two. See where the energy shows up in your body when you bring your intention to mind. Does it feel good? Does it feel right? Does it feel "on purpose?" Ask yourself, "is this something I will really do?" Listen for the answer. You'll hear it. And you'll recognize a true intention when it appears. And if you know you're not going to do it, stop talking about it.

Directives for the Week: Continue with your journaling and meditation.

1. Upon waking, make a list of your intentions for the day. Make sure not to make a list of your plans for the day, but your **intentions**. Plans may change, but your intentions will not. Remember: Intentions are **thoughts activated**!

2. Make a list of your global Intentions. Global Intentions are those things that are long term and integral to your purpose

in life. An example of a Global Intention would be to intend a life of service. Another would be to intend to make music a driving force in your life. One Boot Camper decided during Intention Week to compose a piece of music. However, she didn't play an instrument, so she decided to start piano lessons. Her Global Intention required her to create the immediate intention of playing the piano.

3. This week choose a Global Intention from your list and focus on the meaning behind that intention. When you are certain that your intention is clear, choose something that supports the intention and accomplish it. Follow through and see it to its conclusion. Pick something uplifting, something that will energize your Life Force. It doesn't have to be as grand as ending world hunger, but it *does* have to feed your soul.

Don't just flirt with intention, make one and then act on it. Without the action it's nothing more than wishful thinking.

Affirm this throughout the week:

My intentions always manifest.
They climb every hill, ascend every peak.
I back my intention with my Word!

*Keep mindful of your **WORD**!*

WEEK ELEVEN

DAY TWO

Meditation: 10-minute minimum

> *"A good intention clothes itself with power."*
> *Ralph Waldo Emerson*

Sometimes the strongest action we can take is to step into the quiet of our own mind. There we will find not only the answers, but the questions that activate our Beingness. **Allow** yourself to contemplate your highest intentions.

Check in on the chatter in your mind. Join the conversation from a place of observance. Notice what you're thinking about and reflect on the things that come up. Don't force yourself to "do" anything. Just be with yourself and with your thoughts.

Communication: I have noticed that many people hit the wall during Intention Week. They look at their lives and see unfulfilled dreams and empty intentions. That happens. "Shift happens!" And that's exactly what is happening. Whether or not you feel it, it's happening. You are shifting.

If you've come this far and have worked the program, you are shifting. You don't believe me? It doesn't really matter whether you believe me. Do you believe yourself? Do you do what you say you're going to do? Have you followed the program? Have you put one of your intentions into action in the past few days? Are you expecting to complete it and demonstrate it by the next session? That's all that matters in this moment.

Do you understand what an intention is? Can you make one, and follow through, so that it doesn't wind up in the abyss of "just thinking?"

I think, therefore I am.
I intend; therefore I do!

- What have you decided to intend into being this week? What steps have you taken to manifest your intention? Write it down. Refer to it as you make your way through the week. Reinforce your desire to fulfill your intention. Become a person of your **word,** especially in your relationship to yourself.

- How is your spiritual practice coming? Are you meditating more? Are you continuing with your morning journaling?

- What are your intentions regarding the remainder of Boot Camp? Write them out and see how well you accomplish them.

- For group work, share your intention with the others. Become accountable to the group for demonstrating your intention. Keep mindful of your time allotment. No cross-talking.

Intention: What really separates an intention from a wish is the energy that accompanies an intention. It is defined as an "active purpose." The action inherent in the intention would support it being manifest through our willingness to act on purpose. As one Boot Camper put it, "I know when I have an intention and when I'm just blowing smoke. When I have an intention, it happens." And it really is as simple as that. What we must do is program ourselves to know at the start whether we're steeped in intention or if we're just blowing smoke.

Attention/Accountability: Are you blowing smoke or are you intentionally doing the work? If you aren't doing the work, ask yourself why? Don't beat yourself up, just intend to do it differently. And then, as my grandmother would say, DO IT!

- Journal and meditate.

- Make a list of your Global Intentions.

- Choose one action to forward your intention and DO IT!

Do you believe that you deserve to live life to the fullest as the highest expression of your True Self? You're the only one who can make that happen.

Quotes from Boot Camp

"I cannot believe how many things I thought were intentions that were just hopes and plans and ... I won't use the word I wanna use. Yes I will – it's just a bunch of crap. I still didn't use the word I wanted to use."

"I think I listen more to what other people intend for me."

"Without intentions I can avoid disappointment. That's what first came to me. I guess I'm going to have to look at that!"

"It seems like my intentions are based on what I 'think' I can accomplish. If I know I have control over something, then I know I can do it. It's the other things that seem out of reach, so I don't intend anything about them."

"I think what I really intend is to not intend anything specific."

Continue with this week's directives!

***A meal is eaten one bite at a time,
otherwise, you might choke.***

Do the work ... LIVE THE RESULTS!

WEEK TWELVE
SELF-ESTEEM/RESPECT

WEEK TWELVE

DAY ONE

Meditation: Expanding our awareness of Spiritual Practice.

"It isn't until you come to a Spiritual understanding of who you are,
not necessarily a religious feeling, but deep down, the Spirit within,
that you can begin to take control of your life."
Oprah Winfrey

One of the benefits of meditation is that it centers us in our power to create. When we get in touch with our True Nature, it is that much easier to let loose and just DO. **_Intentions_** become realized and purpose becomes activated.

Today, take a moment before you begin meditating to set your **_Intention_**. When you clearly state your purpose, the Universe responds with precise clarity. Start taking control of your life by taking control of your mind and **Allowing** Life to do what it does perfectly, respond to your **_intentions_** with a resounding **YES**!

Communication: This week, you were asked to choose something to further one of your Global Intentions and then DO IT. Were you able to accomplish this? What was the **_intention_** you chose? Was it something easy, simple, fun? Often, one of our biggest stumbling blocks is our creative way of putting things in categories. We think that curing a cold is easy while curing cancer is difficult. We decide that we have the ability to find a parking space when we need one ("good parking karma"), but we somehow make finding a job or the perfect mate hard to do. We label some things as easy and others as difficult. The Truth is, it's all the same. Easy, hard, it's just a matter of perspective.

"There is no great and no small
to the soul that maketh all."
Ralph Waldo Emerson

This is one of my favorite quotes. How wonderful it is to develop the mindset that whatever I decide to do is equally as doable as anything else. There's nothing to say that this thing is hard and something else is easier. I'm the only one who decides that. And I choose to decide whatever suits my needs. So, if I am contemplating a trip to Bali or a jog in the park, they are equally as doable. I just have to be clear of my *intentions* and let the Universe provide me with the details. Of course, it all comes from my willingness to act on my *intention*.

One Boot Camper shared that he felt like a hamster in a wheel. He runs and runs, trying to get where he's going, but he never gets anywhere other than where he is. Doesn't matter what the *intention* is, he's standing still. He wanted something to help him break free from the wheel.

In acting there's a thing called your "super objective." It's what a character wants overall from the story being told. This super objective is at the heart of every decision and behavior. It's the same with *intention*. At the heart of every specific *intention* is a super intention or Global Intention. If my overall objective in life is to succeed, then each of my specific *intentions* is going to be motivated by my Global Intention. Often what we find, however, is that much of our lives are being played out in conflict. I say I want happiness, but my specific *intentions* don't match my super intention.

- What have you identified as your super intention on a global scale, meaning your whole life picture?

- Look at your specific *intention* for the week. Did it take you a step closer to accomplishing your Global Intention? Did it compliment your "purpose" in life?

- Write down the history of how your ***intention*** manifested. Go back through the week and chronicle the steps you took to succeed at demonstrating your result. List the challenges, stumbling blocks (if any), and those times when it all just flowed.

- If for some reason, you did not succeed, still chronicle your week's activities regarding your ***intention*** as listed above.

- If you are in a group, share your thoughts. (Keeping mindful of your time allotment). No cross-talking.

Remember, ***intentions*** are thoughts activated. If you find yourself not acting on something, chances are you haven't really set an ***intention***. It's time to take a good look at what we say we want in life. Have we set an ***intention*** or just hoped for something good? If we've set an ***intention***, then we are making decisions.

> *"A real decision is measured by the fact that you've taken new action.*
> *If there's no action, you haven't truly decided."*
> Tony Robbins

What have you decided? What are your ***intentions?*** Make sure you know and then make double sure you act on them.

Intention: This week's Intention is ***Self-Esteem/Respect.***

> *"If you put a small value on yourself,*
> *rest assured that the world will not raise your price."*
> Unknown

On the heels of ***Intention*** comes Self-Esteem. One would imagine that if they knew the true depth of their Inner Being, their self-esteem would be concretized (set in stone). It seems that if we dissected every challenge down to its smallest particle of fact, we would ultimately come up with one niggling commonality. We don't know who we are.

"The bondage of humanity must be
a result of our ignorance of our True Nature."
Ernest Holmes

Do you know your True Nature? Or as Cyndi Lauper sang, "your true colors shining through"? What are your True Colors? Do you go within to define who you are? What is your estimate of yourself? How deeply do you respect yourself? Most of us build our estimation of people out of what they accomplish. We can point to modern day figures who demand respect and attention. They have succeeded in ways that are admirable. We like what they have to say. We like what they do. We see in them what we would like to see in ourselves. They have confidence, charisma, success, and it is well founded.

When you see someone who is successful, it is right to conclude that they are clear on success. When you see someone who is happy, it is correct to conclude that they are clear on happiness. I am talking about people who we know are happy and successful, not those we think possess these qualities. Seeing someone on the cover of *People*, smiling away with the new love of their life, doesn't mean a thing. Many times, it isn't even the love of their life. I know a lot of these people and what you read is rarely accurate. So, it's not celebrities that I'm referring to – it's the people in your life that you can point to and say, "he's happy," "she's successful."

During one Boot Camp, a young woman had a meltdown with regard to what she thought of herself. She was having success as an actor, booking television guest spots and shooting commercials. She knew that she was good but just couldn't break through to the next level of success. When she started looking at what she really thought of herself, she became depressed. She didn't believe she was "worthy." Her past constantly reminded her that she was just "acting" as if she deserved it. And since she was a good actor, she could fool even herself into thinking she was doing fine. But she wanted more than just "fine." She wanted her True Colors.

What we are on the inside manifests itself on the outside in perfect proportion. We cannot escape it. If you want to know what you think about yourself, look around at your life. It will never fail to accurately exhibit a litmus test of your self-esteem. If you have a high respect for yourself, it will show in how you live your life.

Respect is defined as, "esteem expressed toward a person." In the case of one's respect for self, therefore, it would seem that self-esteem is linked to respect for the self. When I respect myself, I make decisions differently. When I am rich with self-esteem, I walk confidently though each day knowing that my **Word** is the law of my life. I think Aretha Franklin had it correct when she sang, "**R.E.S.P.E.C.T –
find out what it means to me.**" Until we uncover our own level of self-respect/self-esteem, we might be acting up a storm while the demons of low self-worth hide comfortably in the corner manipulating the performance of our life.

__Attention/Accountability__: Pay *attention* this week to how you treat yourself. Pay *attention* as well to how you treat others. It's a mirror to what you think of yourself. Often, I will hear people explain that they have no problem being nice to others. They like being supportive and helpful, giving of their time and *attention*. If there's something that someone needs, they are always there. But, in fact, if we cannot be there for ourselves, we really aren't there for anyone else because we do not show up as a fully realized person. We might be able to provide services, but the greatest gift we can ever give someone is to share with them our commonality, our Oneness. To do that we have to know who we are in the True Nature of Life.

__Directives for the Week__: Continue with your morning journal and meditation.

1. Keep an ongoing list of what your life looks like in terms of self-esteem and respect. Have I built a life that is worthy of who I am? What things can I do in my present situation to build up and nurture my self-esteem? What things can

I eliminate from my life that do not respect my self-worth? Make note of these things throughout each day. In the evening, read over what you've gathered and check in on what you feel about what you are uncovering. What decisions can you make to move yourself forward? Write them out.

2. Do one thing for yourself each day that honors who you are. It could be a special meal, time alone, a walk on the beach, going through an old steamer trunk looking at pictures. Whatever it is, do it.

3. Print out the affirmation, I AM WORTH IT, and put it where you will see it throughout the day. Let it remind you that you are in control of your life and that you are worthy of any and all success, prosperity, health, creativity and love you could possibly imagine ... and then some.

*"We do not believe in ourselves until
someone reveals that deep inside us is valuable,
worth listening to, worthy of our trust, sacred to our touch.
Once we believe in ourselves, we can risk curiosity,
wonder, spontaneous delight or any experience
that reveals the human spirit."*
e.e. cummings

The world will value you, as you do!

WEEK TWELVE

DAY TWO

**Meditation**: I am worth it!

When I look within, I see the light.
It illuminates the Truth that I am worth my highest thought.
I continue on this journey of self-knowing,
recognizing that my life is limitless.

I AM WORTH IT!

Take these words into your meditation. Notice any resistance to the phrase, "I Am Worth It!" _**Allow**_ yourself to be at peace with your feelings while gently nudging yourself back to the Truth that you are, indeed, worth it.

**Communication**: Behind most failure is a belief of unworthiness. "I am worth it," although simple in thought, is a powerful measure of self-esteem. When you say this to yourself, what do you feel? Do you feel silly? Does it feel like the truth? Does it work for some things and not others? One Boot Camper wrote: _"I am certainly worth a nice car, but a new career where I call the shots seems out of reach."_

Does that sound familiar? I often hear people in Boot Camp express frustration at not being able to move forward on certain issues. What we are taught to do is look at the facts and see what we can change, or what we can overcome. It is very easy to point the finger and see something external as the issue. We say "that" is in my way, when the Truth is, YOU are in your way. We get to experience whatever we can consciously equal. In order to equal what we deserve, we must first know who we are.

"Self esteem is the reputation we acquire with ourselves."
Nathaniel Branden

- Looking at your life, what do you conclude about your self-esteem? Do you treat yourself as though you are worth it? Are your decisions based on a healthy assessment of who you are?

- How do you feel when you are treating yourself to something nurturing?

- Are you willing to write down what you really think about yourself? Take some time to get clear. Try to eliminate the B.S. and get to the heart of the matter. Then you can get to work on creating a Belief System that reinforces a healthy knowingness of Self-Esteem/Respect.

- For group work, share your thoughts with one another. (Keeping mindful of your time allotment). No cross-talking.

Intention: What is healthy self-esteem? How important is self-respect? A healthy self-esteem is the difference between success and failure. The importance of self-respect is likened to the importance of air to the lungs. Without air, we experience lung failure. Without self-esteem and self-respect, we will continually find ourselves gasping for air, struggling to succeed at the very basics of life.

"How am I supposed to change my self-esteem
when I know 'my story?' I can't change the past and it certainly
shows me a bleak view of who and what I am."

This was shared one morning during Boot Camp. I immediately reminded the person that who they are and what they are has nothing to do with who they were and what they were. It's just a "story" and it happened in the past, which is why it's just a "story." The past isn't the problem. The "story" isn't even the problem. We all have a "Story." You can't be alive without having a "Story" of some kind.

But our reaction to our "Story" is the key to rebooting our self-esteem. So what if you don't respect what you did in the past? Who cares if you've failed miserably at everything you've attempted up to this point? Clearly you didn't know who you were. You "thought" you were what you did, instead of realizing that who you are, who you *truly* are, is unchangeable. If you don't like the past, do the present differently. Don't get caught up in what you used to do. Become the person who **USED to do it that way**. Become the person who now knows better. And you *do* **KNOW BETTER** – because you now know who you are.

I'd like to add one more thing about self-esteem and self-respect. If you are holding on to anything from the past that you need to forgive, either with yourself or with another, do it now. We cannot love ourselves if we are holding anything against ourselves. And if we are holding anything against another, we are holding it against our self. That is just common sense. You are in opposition with your True Nature if you hold any resentment or guilt from the past. So forgiving is something you need to do. Get to work on it.

However, forgiving doesn't mean allowing past behavior to continue. Unfortunately, when some people show you who they are, they aren't in touch with their True Colors. They are in a state of human confusion. And while they're in that state of confusion, there is no reason to have them over for dinner. Forgiving them their confusion is essential to your own self-esteem, but there is no reason to accept their behavior. I like the idea of "when necessary, forgive and move on."

Attention/Accountability:

1. Are you continuing to write in the mornings, keeping *your Word* in the forefront of your mind?

2. Are you making lists of things in your life that are a direct result of your self-esteem and respect for yourself?

3. Have you taken time to do something for yourself each day that nurtures your self-esteem?

4. Have you placed the affirmation I AM WORTH IT in a location where you are continually reminded of the Truth of your Nature, your True Colors?

5. Are you actively forgiving everyone and everything and starting with a clean slate?

Quotes from Boot Camp

"It's so easy to think the best of someone else. Actually, it's not too hard to think the worst of them either. I do better with myself when I have something to judge me for."

"I think I just need to change self-esteem to Self-Esteem. Capitalizing the S in Self helps remind me that there's something in me bigger than all the crap."

"I don't think I've been too nice with myself."

"I'm willing to respect myself now, but it's hard to respect who I used to be. I guess I have to get to work on forgiveness."

"I like the idea, 'forgive and move on.' Now I feel like I can forgive someone and still keep my distance. I used to think that 'not forgiving them' was how I kept them away."

"I need to start respecting the 'little things' because they add up to the 'big things.'"

"Wouldn't it be great if everyone loved themselves? It would make life so much easier."

Continue with this week's directives!

YOU ARE WORTH IT!

Do the work ... LIVE THE RESULTS!

WEEK THIRTEEN
COMMUNICATION

WEEK THIRTEEN

DAY ONE

Meditation: Clearing the path to Self-Esteem

> *"What lies behind us and what lies before us*
> *are tiny matters compared to what lies within us."*
> *Ralph Waldo Emerson*

Within you is the infinite wisdom of the Universe, the overflowing creativity of the ages and the soothing, peaceful love of a quantum field of energy. **Allow** this to be your Truth as you quiet the mind and journey the path to your highest self.

> *"This is love: to fly toward a secret sky,*
> *to cause a hundred veils to fall each moment.*
> *First to let go of life. Finally, to take a step without feet."*
> *Jalal ad-Din Rumi*

Take a step, during these next 10 minutes, to allow yourself to drop whatever veils continue covering your authentic self. Take a step without form into the silence of your mind. Allow yourself the pleasure of your true Self.

Communication: This week, you were asked to take time each day to honor yourself. Did you find things that strengthened your Life Force? Did you respect yourself enough to take time out of your busy schedule to refill your mind/body? When you came face-to-face with the affirmation "I Am Worth It," how did it make you feel? Do you find yourself giving over to the higher idea of Self? Or are you still resistant to thinking of yourself as something separate from your past? Are you living in the present moment, fully realized and realizing that you are at choice in each moment to step into your greatness? Are you finding that you've created a life worthy of who you are? If not, are you ready to do so?

"Above all, be true to yourself.
And if you cannot put your heart in it,
take yourself out of it."
Hardy D. Jackson

How hard would it be for you to do only those things that made you happy? Does that sound like a fantasy world? Is it something you could believe in? Without a belief in the possibility of such a world, it will never come into being. Well, I do believe in such a world. And the initiating factor is to start, right here in this moment, to commit to things that make you happy. Conversely, you must begin to weed out those things that detract from your well-being. We cannot develop healthy self-esteem or respect ourselves any better if we continually live lives that are not up to our own standards. It really is time to stop "surviving" and start "thriving." To do that we have to first decide to live up to our True Nature.

- Take a look at the list of things that contribute to your self-esteem and those that do not. Begin to target those things that no longer serve you. Make an informed, conscious list of those things that fill you up, make you happy, and infuse passion into your life.

- If you are in a group, make a commitment to those around you to continue staying on course, building your Energy Circle out of those things that reinforce healthy self-esteem and respect. Share those things with the group. (Keeping mindful of your time allotment.) No cross-talking.

Toward the end of Boot Camp one morning, someone said, "I think I should quit my job. It doesn't fulfill me, and I have no passion when I'm at work." Even though she wasn't financially stable enough to quit, she was in a place of uncertainty about whether to take the leap. She asked if I thought she should quit. I told her that the very fact that she was asking for my opinion meant that she was not really ready to quit her job. It wasn't that she didn't mean what she was saying about the job itself. But she was not at the point yet where she could quit her job for the right reason, thereby creating the next experience from her newfound self-image.

She knew what wasn't working in her life, but she was still unsure of what was working. Once she got clear on who she was/is, she not only quit her job, but ended up buying the company she was so unhappy with. I have a feeling that the employees of that company are much happier today thanks to their new owner uncovering her True Colors. What are you ready to uncover? Put it in your journal and give it some Attention.

Intention: This week's Intention is Communication.

> *"Tell me and I'll forget.*
> *Show me and I'll remember.*
> *Involve me and I'll understand."*
> *Confucius*

Since communication is an important part of Spiritual Boot Camp, it makes sense that we dedicate a week to what it means in the "bigger picture." How do we communicate to the world around us, to ourselves and to the impersonal law of cause and effect? What are we putting out there? Because whatever we are "putting out" is "coming back," whether we like it or not. That's how it works.

Communication is not just about the words we choose. It's smart to always be mindful of what words we decide to use in life, how we present ourselves and what we are attempting to accomplish with any communication. However, it's what's behind the words that constitute the substance of what we are truly communicating.

How many times have you had a conversation with someone, heard every word, and yet simultaneously heard the deafening sound of their "inner dialogue," the subtext to what was being said? We all know the saying, "actions speak louder than words." It's true. We communicate with action far more effectively than with words.

Sticks and stones may break my bones,
but names will never hurt me.

And yet, what we communicate to someone can be extremely hurtful. Passive-aggressive behavior has crept into our society with such alarming regularity; it has almost become acceptable behavior. Sometimes people aren't even aware that they are doing it. Just the other day someone was explaining to a group of people that she was disappointed with them. She went out of her way to say that this group's behavior was "totally understandable," but that she had worked with another group who was "open and positive and always willing to figure out a solution." She indicated that this group was not. When she was questioned on why she felt this group was not open or positive, she quickly stated that she never said they weren't, just that the other group was. And it was all couched with such "respectful" B.S. that I was left feeling uncomfortable.

Do you communicate from an Authentic Self? What do you think you communicate to the world on an ongoing basis? How are your words influenced by what you think, feel and ultimately believe? Do you say what you think or do you "couch" it in a way that feels "safe?" Do you let people know how you truly feel, or are you willing to let a feeling of vagueness surround a situation?

What is being communicated to you from the world around you? Are people generally straightforward with you, or do they beat around the bush? How much passive-aggressive dialogue clutters up your day? Are you happy with the level of communication in your life? How often do you use "catch phrases" to communicate? Catch phrases are things that you use to avoid communication or to stall for time to think. Often, these are things that we say out of habit – and most of the time aren't even true.

I discovered during an earlier Boot Camp that I used the catch phrase "The truth is ... ." I started catching myself using it all over the place. I no longer use that catch phrase, only on special occasions.

Attention/Accountability: Pay attention this week to how you communicate. Listen to the words you use, the catch phrases you utilize in order not to communicate or stall for time. Notice when you are saying things in direct conflict to what you are feeling. Also take note on how the world is communicating to you. Notice the way people talk, what they convey beyond the words. Look at their body language, their eye contact, whether or not they smile while they're with you. There's a lot to pick up, we just have to be willing to actively notice.

Directives for the Week: Continue with your morning journal and meditation.

1. First thing each morning, check in to see how you are communicating with yourself. What are you telling yourself in those first few moments each day? Journal from this point of view.

2. Spend each day being mindful of how and what you are communicating to the world around you. Conversely, pay attention to what's coming at you from others. Listen to their words but, more importantly, tap into what's behind the words.

3. Make a list of all the catch phrases you use during the course of each day.

"If you just communicate you can get by.
But if you skillfully communicate, you can work miracles."
Jim Rohn

Choose words wisely, choose Beliefs even more so!

WEEK THIRTEEN

DAY TWO

**Meditation:** A communication to and from Spirit

> _"Being articulate is not a facility of language_
> _but a fidelity to vision. And so, we are all articulate_
> _when finding the courage to say what we see."_
> _Mark Nepo_

An important part of communication is the ability to say what you see and hear. Take the next few moments to tune into the silence in such a way that you hear exactly what is there for you to hear and see what is yours to see. Start with the following question:

What wants to happen here?

Now **allow** the Universe to communicate to you through you.

**Communication:** What have you been communicating to yourself thus far this week? What comes up first thing in the morning? How does the world seem to communicate to you? Are people direct, cautious, kind? Have you caught yourself shifting into catch phrases such as, "I don't know," "I know what you mean," "Why bother," and whatever else just comes out without thinking? It's maddening sometimes when you actually allow yourself to notice it. I recently realized, that there were times when I would put "I don't know" in front of an answer just to take a moment to figure out what I wanted to say. How confident do you think it looks to respond to a question with "I don't know" and then give the answer? What am I communicating? Perhaps I want to come off as someone who isn't a know-it-all. Maybe I want people to know that I allow for opposing thought. Whatever the reason, I realized that it would be much better to use the correct words for what I'm thinking in the moment. "I don't know" needs to be reserved for when I actually don't know.

I remember when my twins were almost 2. They would struggle to say what they wanted with words they had heard but perhaps didn't understand. One day my son was trying to say he wanted to go swimming and he kept saying, "Fool!" I thought he was a little young for put downs, so I wasn't too insulted. Finally, after yelling "FOOL" for a few moments, he pulled me over to the window and pointed to the pool. When the wrong words get in the way, action is always best. Don't tell me! Show me! That's good communication.

- What catch phrases have you caught?

- Looking around at those within your Energy Circle, do you think there's an authenticity to your communication?

- How well do you hear what you are communicating to yourself? Do you listen to what you say, not only in the words you use but in the intentions behind the words? Do others listen to you? If not, do you know why?

- Write out your thoughts on these questions in your journal. Then take a moment to read what you wrote. What are you communicating to yourself?

- For group work, share the "aha moments" you've been having. (Keeping mindful of your time allotment.) No cross-talking.

Intention: There are so many different levels of communication; if we were to experience them all at once, it would be quite maddening. Very often people aren't even aware of what is "behind" a specific line of thought or conversation. How many times have you had an in-depth conversation with an intimate friend and when you reach the end of it, neither of you are aware of what you'd been talking about for hours?

One Boot Camper shared that she and her husband have a great relationship. They are able to talk about anything. They have an agreement to share their feelings, no matter how difficult it may be for the other. One day, her husband told her that he was attracted to a co-worker. Her response was, "I don't need to hear that." "But we agreed to tell one another everything," he said. To which she replied, "Only tell me if the attraction leads to something concrete. Other than that, I'll just stick with the delusion that I'm the only woman you find attractive." We all laughed at this, but it does bring up a good point: Good communication depends on our willingness to allow it in.

This week gives us a good opportunity to see if there is anything we're not willing to "hear," or let in.

Attention/Accountability:

1. Have you continued to journal this week, focusing on the first thing you communicate to yourself in the morning?

2. Are you keeping up with your meditation practice?

3. Are you making a list of your catch phrases, paying attention to your own communication skills and what might be behind the words?

4. How is the world communicating to you? Are you doing the work to hear what is being communicated behind the words of others?

Quotes from Boot Camp

"I occasionally say, 'You know what,' before I say something. It's like I'm asking myself to respond. That's weird and I never thought about it until now."

"My catch phrase? 'The thing is ...' It was so bad that it started to precede everything I would say. It got so bad that for a while I couldn't respond to

anything because I was too busy stopping my catch phrase from popping out."

"Communication would be a lot easier if you just didn't have to communicate with other people."

"I feel like I communicate, people just don't always want to hear it."

"What's the healthy ratio between listening and speaking?"

Continue with this week's directives!

*"Communication leads to community,
that is, to understanding, intimacy and mutual valuing."
Rollo May*

Do the work ... LIVE THE RESULTS!

WEEK FOURTEEN
FEELINGS

WEEK FOURTEEN

DAY ONE

Meditation: An infinite communication with Universal Wisdom

When I look for You ... my eyes delight.
When I listen for You ... there is music.
When I hunger for You ... the harvest is sweet.
When I know You ... I know myself.

Allow your mind to empty of the relative facts. Sink deeply into the Absolute Truth of your Inner Being. It all begins with quieting the mind. It's where you will find your Authentic Self.

Communication: How do you communicate to the world? What comes out of your mouth most of the time? What goes into your head most of the time? Do people usually understand you? What percentage doesn't? How often do you have to repeat yourself? Are you someone who makes things clear, or do you leave things hanging? Are you okay with confusion? I know that sounds like a silly question. I mean, who would be okay with confusion? I think we spend a lot of time in confusion because we don't want to commit to being clear.

"I think I keep things nebulous, so I have an escape route."
Boot Camper

I loved this quote from one of our Boot Campers. What we came to, in our session, was that every time communication is nebulous, the outcome matches it perfectly. At some point, someone is going to have to be clear. We only need escape routes when we find ourselves at risk. There's no risk to being truthful (with respect, always with respect).

- Did you find catch phrases that were stand-ins for actual

thoughts and beliefs? What were they, and are you able to eliminate them?

- What came up for you regarding how you communicate to the world? Were you surprised, delighted, confused, annoyed? How do you communicate to the world?

- What do you communicate when you wake up? Have you been able to redirect anything you found to be limiting?

- Put your answers, including your catch phrases, into your journal. It's always a good thing to go back and see where you were and how far you've come.

- This past week was a very full week. Check in to see if you did the required work. Stay mindful of the catch phrases you use to detach from communication.

- Group work: Share your catch phrases, if you found any, and any "aha moments" you had regarding your communication. (Keeping mindful of your time allotment). No cross-talking.

Intention: This week's Intention is Feelings.

> *"I've learned that people will forget what you said,*
> *people will forget what you did,*
> *but people will never forget how you made them feel."*
> *Maya Angelou*

There is a misconception that we feel based on what is going on around us. We often hear people ask us, "How does that make you feel?" We enter into long, often draining, conversations about our feelings in relation to this or that, or any number of things we blame for our feelings. Years and years of therapy can be spent trying to get to the feelings.

But I think we might do better to consciously decide what we feel in the first place, and then move forward from there.

I remember going to a new movie with a bunch of friends, and I won't name the movie. But suffice to say that it was a highly-anticipated musical. In the dark of the theater we all experienced the same screen, the same dialogue, the same actors singing the same songs. We were all at the "same" movie. When we came out, you would have thought the skies had opened and we were experiencing a modern-day "Tower of Babel."

I was trying to explain how a certain part brought tears to my eyes, when one of our group started laughing. He said the only tears that came to his eyes were from the air conditioning hitting his tear ducts – his eyes had been popped open so wide from his disbelief of how anyone could take a perfectly good stage musical and destroy it like that. WOW! What happened? Same movie, different people.

Feelings come from what someone brings to the party,
not from the party itself.

What I have noticed in my life is that every time I blame something or someone for making me feel a certain way, I wind up with more of the same feeling, and less of who I am. In the end, I am responsible for what I feel. When I feel good, I own it. When I feel bad, I change it. It's that simple.

We choose our feelings. They don't choose us.

Attention/Accountability: This week, pay attention to how you feel in any given situation. Notice your tendency to "pinning" it on something or someone other than yourself. Pay attention to what you bring to the party. You're there, so you might as well enjoy it.

Every time you feel the urge to "blame" someone for making you feel a certain way, take control of the feeling, not the person who you decided is responsible for creating the feeling. If you're feeling it, own it.

By owning it, you recognize that you have the power to change it. By doing this we eliminate the buttons that we continually accuse people of pushing. If you haven't rid yourself of these pesky buttons yet, now would be a good time to do so. It's Feelings Week, after all.

Directives for the Week: Continue with your morning journal. Try to add some extra time this week to your meditation.

1. First thing each morning, ask yourself, "How do I feel?" Decide, in the moment, if this is good or bad. Recognize that you can go with the "flow" or redirect the current. Your choice!

2. Ask yourself throughout the day, "What am I feeling?" Trace your feelings back to your own thoughts/beliefs. Don't judge yourself or your feelings. Notice them, own them, and take charge of them. When you can trace a feeling back to something specific, write it in your journal for future reference. You'd be surprised how many patterns repeat themselves, conjuring up the same feelings each time.

3. At the end of each day, in a very short sentence, summarize what you felt during Feelings Week.

*"A man sooner or later discovers
that he is the master-gardener of his soul,
the director of his life."*
James Allen

*"A good psychological balance is struck
when the will and the emotions are rightly poised.
That is, when the intellect first decides
what the emotions are to respond to."*
Ernest Holmes

It's a decision and it's yours to make.
What do I want to feel today?

Feel good – it's who you are!

WEEK FOURTEEN

DAY TWO

Meditation: Pay Attention to how meditation makes you feel. See if you can expand on the feeling by taking it with you and using it throughout your day.

Allow the following words to take you into your silence.

> *"Oh, for a tongue to express the Wonders*
> *which the thought reveals!*
> *Oh, for some Word to comprehend*
> *the boundless idea!*
> *Would that some voices were sweet enough*
> *to sound the harmony of Life.*
> *But within, in that vast realm of thought*
> *where the Soul meets God,*
> *the Spirit knows.*
> *I will listen to that voice, and it will tell me*
> *of Life, of Love and Unity."*
> *Ernest Holmes*

Communication: How have you been feeling? Are you noticing that your feelings are actually a result of how you approach life? We can decide how we're going to feel in any given situation, not by forcing ourselves to feel a certain way, but by strengthening our beliefs in such a way that we orchestrate the symphony that is our life.

If I know that I am always going to see the good in any situation, then my feelings are filtered through that belief. If I know that there is evil lurking out there to "get me," then my feelings will jump out at me like a ghoul in a horror flick. As much as I like "Psycho," I don't want to shower in that house.

"The trick is in what one emphasizes.
We either make ourselves miserable, or we make ourselves happy.
The amount of work is the same."
Carlos Castaneda

- Look at what you have written thus far about your feelings. Is there a pattern?

- Have you been able to trace your feelings back to a belief and restructure it to create the feelings you want?

- For group work, talk about the communication of the Boot Camp thus far. (Keeping mindful of your time allotment). No cross-talking.

Intention: "Feeling patterns" can be hard to root out. The very nature of the feeling is usually so prominent that the pattern takes a back seat. Each time we visit the feeling, we are so caught up in "it" that "it" feels almost new. But it isn't. It was caused by a chain reaction to a core belief and can be overturned by a firm decision to react differently. However, the decision needs to be made BEFORE the next event happens, causing the "feeling pattern" to kick in again. You get to decide right now, in this moment, that you are the creator and curator of your feelings.

What we sometimes forget is that we have options. Instead of anger, we can choose peace. Instead of blame, we might choose forgiveness. Sadness can be reframed as joy. Just recently, I facilitated a memorial service where the family of a very dear and loving woman came together to mourn her death. She was a very forward-thinking woman who had left her religious roots to pursue New Thought alternatives. She made it very clear in her will that she wanted the service to reflect where her religious journey had taken her. My job was to respect her wishes, as well as create a respectful atmosphere and comfort the family members, all very devout Catholics. What started out as sadness and apprehension for the family quickly turned to celebration and joy. The core belief that we are all One and that love must always be at the center of life reframed the entire situation.

What we can choose to know is that, rather than reacting to something, we can always figure out what's at the center of it all. A mind steeped in the understanding that Good is at the center of all things will always fare better than the alternative. Feelings of good will follow a belief in Good. All feelings have their base in some core belief.

Change your BELIEF, change your FEELING.

Attention/Accountability:

1. Are you taking the morning time necessary to center your mind and focus your day?

2. Are you checking in at night and journaling a short sentence to wrap up the day's feelings?

3. Have you begun to take charge of your mind by tracing your feelings back to the beliefs that created them?

How do you feel about where you are in this Boot Camp? Trace it back.

Quotes from Boot Camp

"You mean I can't blame my mother anymore? That doesn't feel right. I'm joking, of course. Sort of."

"I've excavated this gnawing 'feeling' that things just might not work out for me. I seem to bring it to every party."

"My wife told me that I don't like 'feeling' things. But I think I just don't like feeling 'bad' things."

"For years I thought I was just an emotional person. I thought a good crying jag was essential to healthy living. Not that I don't still cry occasionally. I just don't consider it a pastime anymore."

"I guess the real issue is that I haven't decided that I have control of my feelings."

Continue with this week's directives! Make a decision to take control.

"It's a new dawn, it's a new day, it's a new life ... FEELING GOOD!"
Leslie Bricusse

Do the work ... LIVE THE RESULTS!

WEEK FIFTEEN
JUDGMENT

WEEK FIFTEEN

DAY ONE

Meditation: Take this time today to increase your awareness of the present moment. Ask yourself: Right now, what am I feeling?

Allow your thoughts to slip away. In their place, again ask the following question:

Right now, what am I feeling?

As you enter this sacred time you have reserved for yourself, continue to empty your mind by again calling forth the question:

Right now, what am I feeling?

Allow yourself to explore the feelings as they come forward. Don't identify yourself with them, but notice them as they appear and pass through.

Communication: "Feelings Week" is always an interesting time for Boot Campers. Waking up and asking ourselves, "How do I feel?" requires a certain amount of willingness to be honest and daring. There can be an underlying sense of "doom" in one's unconscious mind that, over time, becomes second nature. What happens then is that all of life is filtered through this "veil" and the picture is always out of focus. And there are many veils to choose from.

When you first wake up in the morning is the perfect time to check in and see, "How do I feel?" One Boot Camper noticed that his "feeling" was somehow linked to the weather. He recognized that, if it was a sunny, warm morning, he could pop right out of bed and jump into his day. If it were cold and damp, he would creak off the mattress, bones stiff and brittle, and slowly get the day going. It had nothing to do with health, he assured me. It was all mental. So, he started jumping out of bed in the morning, regardless of the weather. It worked. He took charge of his feelings and consequently his body.

There are many reasons for us to feel the way we feel. In order to understand our feelings, we need to be aware of what we feel and why, and active in our approach to take control. When we actively take control of our feelings, we begin to see that we are at choice. I can choose to feel good in the face of anything. Dr. Tom Costa, the founding pastor of the Spiritual Center of the Desert in Palm Desert, in a brilliant moment of inspiration, suggested that we add these words to our affirmations:

NO MATTER WHAT!

No matter what I am feeling, I will not give up my right to choose. No matter what is going on in my life, I will not forget who I am. No matter what seems to be standing in my way, I will always remember that there is good for me to have.

I cannot tell you how often I use this phrase in my life. Whenever I start to feel overwhelmed or uncertain, I remember who I am, what I am capable of and I look straight into the fire and claim, NO MATTER WHAT. Try it, it works.

- Look at what you wrote each night this week. What was your "feelings" journey like? Did you recognize any "veils?" Have you stripped them away?

- Did you notice yourself blaming or pinning your feelings on people and situations outside of yourself?

- Were you able to trace your feelings back to a core belief?

- Group work: Be fearless in sharing your feelings from

the week. (Keeping mindful of your time allotment). No cross-talking.

When we become clear that we are always choosing our feelings, we tap into a personal power that is without limit. One Boot Camper put it this way, "I used to feel like a victim. I thought I was feeling what I was supposed to feel." She went on to tell us that she would always get into relationships with guys who would take control of her life, spend her money, and ultimately leave her feeling empty and abused. She would blame the guy. But even more so, she would blame herself. But there was something in her that was sending out invitations to these guys. It was her low self-esteem. Once she recognized her underlying belief that she wasn't worth being treated with respect, she got to work on fixing that belief.

From there, she took charge of her feelings. Eventually, she stopped blaming herself for the past. She started honoring herself for taking the journey and figuring it out once and for all. Months later, after she had completed Boot Camp a second time, she had a relationship with a guy that was pretty good, but as she put it, "not perfect." She decided to end it and they parted as friends. When it was all over, she sent me this quote.

> *"Don't cry because it's over.*
> *Smile because it happened."*
> Dr. Seuss

Feeling is a choice!

Intention: The Intention for this week is Judgment.

> *"Everything that irritates us about others*
> *can lead us to an understanding of ourselves."*
> Carl Jung

This week is all about judgment. But first, let's get clear on just what judgment means. One definition is "the cognitive process of reaching a decision or drawing conclusions." According to Merriam-Webster, it is "the process of forming an opinion or evaluation by discerning and comparing facts." It is also defined as "assigning a value (good or bad) to something." For our purposes, I would like to focus on the idea that a judgment is a drawn conclusion assigning a value of either good or bad to a specific person, place or thing. For me it is the assigning of "value" that turns judgment into a dicey proposition.

So let me ask you right out. Are you a judgmental person? Do you assign "right and wrong," "good and bad," to people or situations? Does your opinion turn to a judgment in the blink of an eye? How are you when it comes to judging yourself? Are you your worst critic?

For our work this week, judgment is that part of opinion that turns ugly. When there is heat around an opinion, there is something more at play. When a situation suddenly becomes personal, we are sinking into judgment. And it's not pretty. It's one thing to send back an entrée in a restaurant. It's another thing altogether to curse the chef for treating you so poorly, shove the table over and storm out the front door. I doubt the chef even knows who you are.

An informed opinion leads us to making clear decisions. A reactive judgment, based on relative facts, colors our thoughts, and most of the time leads only to heartburn.

> *"If you judge people, you have no time to love them."*
> *Mother Teresa*

"I don't think it's possible to go through life without judging people. How would you know who to stay away from?" This was shared one morning during Boot Camp. Most people agreed. In fact, my take on judgment was not very popular. I agreed with Mother Teresa. I consider judgment a waste of time.

Don't get me wrong, I have very strong opinions and I am not easily budged from my decisions. But I put extra work into keeping them impersonal and without "heat." Every time I get involved with whether someone is "good" or "bad," I always end up feeling terrible in the end.

The reason for that is because I believe that all people are innately good, because I believe that all people are, at the deepest level of their soul, One. However, I DO NOT believe that all people are consistently acting from this Oneness. Therefore, it is imperative that we learn how to be discerning while staying non-judgmental. It can be done. I promise.

Recognizing when we are in judgment and when we are in right relation to our opinions is a road to freedom. Ridding ourselves of this time-consuming preoccupation will be a relief. You will feel it for yourself as you work through this week's directives.

Attention/Accountability: This week, pay attention to your inner and outer dialogue. Notice when you are standing in judgment of someone or something. Be very attentive to what your inner dialogue produces in terms of self-judgment. The work this week requires you to go beyond the chatter and to the belief behind the thought. You may think you are merely stating an opinion, but pay attention to how much heat there is in defending your opinion if you need to. That's a sure sign that you just might have drifted into judgment territory.

Also, pay attention to how much judgment is showing up in your world. Make mental notes on who, what, why and when these things occur. Without being judgmental, identify the judgment landscape that makes up your present experience.

Directives for the Week: Continue with your morning journal and meditation.

    1. In each instance, when you catch yourself being judgmental, take the time to turn it around. See through the veil of judgment and impersonalize the facts. If you feel heat, cool

yourself down. Make it an intention for the week to eradicate judgment from your life.

2. Each evening, before you go to bed, rate yourself on a scale of 1 to 10, "was I judgmental today?" If your numbers are high, don't judge yourself.

"Love has no opposite. Duality is man-made."
Ernest Holmes

WEEK FIFTEEN

DAY TWO

Meditation: That place in mind where there is only perfection.

For that place in me
Where there is only light
For that voice in me
Where there is only Truth
For that part of me
Where there is only One

Take a moment to repeat this quote a few times. Allow the words to become your Reality. As the relative world slips away, drift into the Absolute, where you find your place, your voice and your Oneness in the Universe.

Communication: Each week has been designed to release things that no longer serve us and to cultivate a "Spiritual Practice" that aligns us with our highest good. Judgment Week is no exception. There are things that take us down a path of negative results, and being judgmental is one of those paths.

One Boot Camper said that getting rid of her judgmental attitude reminded her of the time she fell into a row of cacti. Every time she thought she'd pulled out all of the thorns, she would find another. As painful as it was to pull the suckers, they had to come out. Otherwise, there would have been an infection.

"Spiritual progress is like detoxification.
Things have to come up in order to be released.
Once we have asked to be healed,
then our unhealed places are forced to the surface."
Marianne Williamson

For the past couple of days, you've been willing to look at what's been coming up in terms of being judgmental.

- What have you found? How have you been rating yourself? What does it bring up for you? Can you distinguish between opinion and judgment?

- How does it feel when you impersonalize the facts? Does it become easier to let go of the judgment? Are you more comfortable with opinions, detaching them from judgment?

- For group work, share your experience, thus far, with becoming aware of judgment and how it plays out in your life. (Keeping mindful of your time allotment). No cross-talking.

Intention: Marianne Williamson has a great point when she writes that spiritual progress is like detoxification. Ridding ourselves of judgment can be painful. Recognizing it within ourselves is the first step to freedom. Once we do, it sometimes comes pouring out of us like water busting through a collapsed dam. As one Boot Camper put it, "I never thought I was judgmental. OH MY GOD, am I judgmental. It makes me wonder what else I've been ignoring." That's the whole point to "Mental Muscle." We focus our energy on specific beliefs, rip them out of their hiding places and replace them with Truth. Voila! My B.S. turns into a healthy Belief System.

Attention/Accountability:

1. Are you taking time to meditate before each session?

2. Are you actively patrolling your mind for moments when you

step into judgment? Are you turning it around or just letting it continue?

3. How does your scale look so far?

4. Are you filling up your journal with your B.S., fearlessly and honestly looking at it and doing what is necessary to eradicate it from your life? If NOT, what's that about?

Remember: Unless you decide to do the work, it probably won't get done. DECIDE!

Quotes from Boot Camp

"When something isn't a duck, calling it a duck doesn't make it a duck. It just makes me stupid!"

"Opinion vs. judgment, that is the question."

"It's hard not to judge people. They give you so much to work with."

"This week should've come earlier. I need a lot of time to work with judgment. It's something I do very well."

"I've noticed this week that when I catch myself judging someone, stop and rethink it, I actually feel better. Who knew?"

"It feels like there's a jury in my head 'judging' me at all times. And I feel like I have no say in the verdict."

"There must be a way to 'dish' without being judgmental. Surely there is. Isn't there? I'm afraid I know the answer."

"It's amazing how much judgment there is in everyday conversation. My friends all seem judgmental to me this week. Is that because I'm imagining it? I don't think so."

Continue with this week's directives!

*"Judgments prevent us from seeing the good
that lies beyond appearances."*
Wayne Dyer

Do the work ... LIVE THE RESULTS!

WEEK SIXTEEN
ACCOUNTABILITY

WEEK SIXTEEN

DAY ONE

Meditation: Tapping into a consciousness of Oneness.

> _If you're ready to take your life in a new direction,_
> _if you're ready to take control of your mind and create a tomorrow_
> _that seems out of reach, if you're ready to put some MENTAL SWEAT_
> _into your Spiritual/Mental creative muscle, then this is for you._

In the final week of Boot Camp, allow yourself to reflect on why you began this journey. Use these operative words to propel you into your "silence."

A – New – Direction

A – New – Me

Communication: You have made it all the way through to Week Sixteen of Spiritual Boot Camp. How does it feel? Have you created a new set of tools to keep you mentally fit? In terms of judgment, where have you landed on your score sheet? Do you know the difference between opinion and judgment? Can you recognize when the heat steps in and drags you down into that dark judgmental abyss?

The funny thing about judgment is that it is often confused for conversation. We are so quick to judge others that it becomes a way of life for some people. Have you ever been dragged into a conversation only to find yourself surrounded by judgmental people, all wanting you to agree with their assessment of someone or something? It's like a drug. You have to have the internal strength to "just say no." Social "dishing," although an unfortunately acceptable part of society, does not move you forward on your spiritual path.

So how did you do?

- Were you aware when you were being judgmental? That's the start, being aware. From awareness comes opportunity to step into action. Were you able to impersonalize the facts and turn them around? Was there a willingness to be less judgmental?

- Were you clear on when you were dealing with opinion and when you stepped into judgment? How did they feel different? What signs were you looking for to distinguish them, one from the other?

- How did you rate on your score sheet? Are you committed to lowering your numbers if they are higher than you want? A good number is zero. No, I'm not kidding.

- In your journal, write how you are feeling about the judgment challenge. Also check in on your feelings about finishing the program.

- Group work: Share your experience during Judgment Week. Be scorchingly honest, there's only one session left. (Keeping mindful of your time allotment). No cross-talking.

Intention: This week's Intention is Accountability.

I remember reading about an interesting tradition of the ancient Romans. Whenever an engineer constructed an arch, as the capstone was hoisted into place, the engineer assumed accountability for his work in the most profound way possible: He stood under the arch.

Are you willing to stand under the arch of your creation? For the past 16 weeks, you have allowed yourself to know yourself. You have fearlessly taken a look at things in your life, qualities of existence, character traits, beliefs and annoying habits. You have put your life under a microscope and examined it day-by-day, moment-by-moment, nuance-by-nuance. In a sense, you have scientifically dissected your personal character and replaced old, archaic, rusty tools with new ones. You have become the creator of your experience. No longer the "reactive" bystander, you are now the Absolute Word in your own life.

I remember when I first heard the saying, "Change your thinking, change your life!" I was instantly hooked. It all made sense to me, in that moment, that my life was playing itself out exactly as I was orchestrating it. I just didn't know I was doing it. Once we find out that we are always at choice, we become responsible for the lives we live. Being accountable is putting your Word into action. You get to decide! You get to choose! You get to create! How great is that?

> *"Thought is the instrument of Mind.*
> *New thoughts create new conditions."*
> Ernest Holmes

It's up to you to create new thoughts. You are at the threshold of a new awareness. Hold yourself accountable to continue the work you have started. Be true to your word. Find new words. Live them! Renew them! Revive them! It's all up to you.

Attention/Accountability: During the next few days, before the final session, read over your journal. Allow the journey of words, ideas and feelings to wash over you with a sense of freedom, ease and accomplishment. Recognize yourself on the page, mindful of who you are in this moment.

Your Journey

The Word
No Complaining
Expectations
Belief
Present
Patience

196   MENTAL MUSCLE

Listen/Hear/Resolve
Boundaries/Priorities
Life Force
Perfectionism
Intention
Self-Esteem
Communication
Feelings
Judgment
Accountability

Directives for the Week: Continue with your morning journal and meditation. How does it feel reaching the conclusion of Boot Camp?

This week, you have one specific directive: Write out a "Spiritual Resume." Apply for the job of <u>God</u>. In your own words and style, communicate to the world why you are right for this job and what skills you have to fulfill the requirements. It doesn't matter what you believe about God, you know what the job would require. Think of George Burns in the movie "Oh, God," or Morgan Freeman in "Bruce Almighty." How would you fare at getting cast as <u>God</u> in today's busy world?

This has always been my favorite part of Spiritual Boot Camp. There are as many ways to accomplish this task as there are Boot Campers. One presented their Spiritual Resume as an original song. Another did a rap that blew us all away. Others wrote comical resumes, and traditional and not-so-traditional renderings. We've had paintings, magic exhibitions, a drum circle, and a recital on a crystal bowl. There is no wrong way to create your Spiritual Resume, other than to not do it.

> *"Every individual has a place to fill in the world,*
> *and is important, in some respect,*
> *whether he chooses to be so or not."*
> *Nathaniel Hawthorne*

Quotes from Boot Camp

"If I get the job as God, things are sure gonna change around here."

"I have to say that I thought I'd be a lot more uncomfortable with the idea of being God than I am. I AM! Why not?"

"Usually, I pad my resume but somehow that doesn't seem right here."

"I couldn't get the image of George Burns out of my head. Then it was Morgan Freeman. I'm working my way to me."

"I'm God, right? So why do I have to apply for the job? I already have it."

Continue with this week's directives!

It's time for you to show the world who you are.

WEEK SIXTEEN

FINAL DAY

Meditation: Try meditating today without a time limit. Allow yourself the time to slow down. Whatever works for you today, do it. You're in charge. It's your intention. It's whatever you want. Be gentle with your mind. Let these words of Kathryn Skatula inform you in some way:

> *When a smile touches our core,*
> *When the eyes connect inside the deepest trust,*
> *When the forest stills us to peace,*
> *When the music moves us to rapture,*
> *When glee paralyzes us into dizzying laughter,*
> *When passion removes the fear of the dance,*
> *When we really love ...*
> *We are one with the angels.*

Communication: In the spirit of a reality TV show pitting contestants against each other, we take you to *So You Think You Are God*. All contestants/Campers have worked very hard to get to where they are, and to exhibit the talents they possess, with such craft and skill they make it look easy. In the interview process, they all told us how they just knew they were the next "God." Some of them were clearly pumping themselves up due to a lack of confidence or some such nonsense. Others were just certain that they would land in the Top Ten. And some still weren't sure, but were willing to give it their best shot.

In this particular show, what the contestants didn't know is that there really isn't a competition. There will never be a No. 1. The "One" title is a conglomerate of the sum total of all its contestants. Each one is needed to provide their "spin" on the Universal Beat. Reality TV competitions work because we witness the magnificence of Spirit flowing through each player. The one who ultimately "wins" (and I use that term in the relative sense only) is the one who, on some level, has tapped into their God-ness.

- How does it feel stepping into your Spiritual Power?

- Are you willing to find good within your every thought?

- Can you own the Truth that you are the creator of your life?

- Will you remain accountable for your actions, remembering that your future is in your own hands?

- Is your Word now part of who you are?

Group Work: If you are doing Spiritual Boot Camp in a group, on this final day, each will read his or her Spiritual Resume out loud. Once everyone has had an opportunity to read, go around the group again and share final thoughts. Cross-talking is permitted, provided it holds the integrity and highest consciousness of the room.

Intention: As the final directive for your Boot Camp journey, you are to find someone you trust, someone who holds you and your journey in high esteem and share your spiritual resume with them. Don't make fun of it or make light of it. Take this seriously. You have unveiled your Authentic Self, and it's time to live it.

FYI, it's OK if your resume is more "fun" oriented. It's great to have fun with it, but don't MAKE fun of it.

Once you've concluded your journey of sharing your spiritual resume finalize the process by journaling what the experience was like. Did you feel silly?

Was it empowering? How was it received? Do you get it yet? You really are the things you were asked at the very beginning of this book ...

Successful

Rich

Talented

Healthy

Happy

... and you already DO have the job. Your only directive from here on out is to ...

ENJOY IT

Congratulations!
You have concluded Spiritual Boot Camp!

I now encourage you to affirm your achievement by returning to your journal and declaring these words as your own.

I, _____, have completed 16 weeks of Spiritual Boot Camp. I hereby make a commitment to myself to adhere to the lessons I have learned. I recognize the Truth that within me is the mental muscle to create greatness. I promise myself to continue my Spiritual Practice by using the tools that work for me, releasing what doesn't work and focusing my attention on my "chosen" intentions.

"There is good for me, and I ought to have it!"
Emma Curtis Hopkins

I say YES to this! I accept my GOOD! I expect my GOOD! I AM my GOOD!

Signed:_____

Date:_____

WHAT NEXT?

After writing this book I was faced with the final task of coming up with a "conclusion." I noticed as I sat down to write that I was balking at the idea of there even being a conclusion. In my mind there is always more. We live in an Infinite Universe that is capable of unlimited creative expression, placing us in the midst of a vast sea of knowledge, understanding and adventure. There is no conclusion, no finish line, just a magnificent journey. When we complete one thing, we are merely ready for the Next.

So I guess the logical question is, what's next? That question can be answered in as many ways as there are grains of sand on a beach. We are pure potentiality ready to explore the horizons of our own individual mind. We are co-creators with this vast quantum field of exquisite possibilities. We can do whatever we decide to do. We can achieve whatever intention we choose to live. We can create whatever we believe we can accomplish. It is up to each of us to take what we know and put it to use. And so, we do.

I honor you for taking this spiritual journey. I honor each and every blessed journey that will follow. I honor where you are in this moment, each moment that brought you to this point, and where you will travel as you move forward. I recognize the greatness in you, recognizing the greatness in me, recognizing the Truth that we are forever One. Namaste'!

ACKNOWLEDGMENTS

*"If the only prayer you said in your whole life
was 'thank you,' that would suffice."*
Meister Eckhart

I want to thank the members of the Board of Trustees at Global Truth Center, past and present, who have called me forth to be a better man, a stronger leader and a Quantum visionary. Through your love, support, and encouragement, I continue my journey to "Love Only, Forgive Everything and Remember Who I Am."

To Rev. Rita Andriello-Feren and Dr. Jonathan Zenz, thank you for jumping into the trenches with me when "Mental Muscle" was only an idea. Your tenacity and wisdom have impacted this book and all it stands for in ways none of us will ever fully realize.

To Dr. Eric Butterworth, my first teacher of the New Thought principles, and to Dr. David J. Walker, my teacher, my mentor and my "linoleum," you taught me to always stand firm in what I know, and I am grateful.

To all Boot Campers, for sharing your desires, intentions, passions, challenges, and fearlessly taking the journey within and facing the Truth, wrestling with the relatives, and crossing the finish line – only to find a new frontier waiting to be explored. Thank you for trusting me and for trusting yourself. Stay true to your "Word!"

To Rev. Suzanne Benoit and Barbara Shane, I thank you both for being the eyes of my soul as you jointly edited and brought the original Mental Muscle into being.

Special thanks also to Brad Kieffer for being the "eyes" of the Anniversary Edition and to Thor Challgren for your ingenuity and relentless passion as you drove this through to completion.

To my son William, who teaches me daily what it means to see the world from a mind that knows how good life is. You inspire me. I am so excited to see what greatness comes from your journey.

To my daughter Nora, whose departure from my life has left a chasm of grief, and yet, an even greater ocean of wisdom in its place. You were, are, and always will be my greatest champion. I feel you everywhere. Always my 5!

Will and Nora, many of my lessons come from what you both have taught me over the years. Thank you ... now and forever.

And last, and certainly most of all, to the man who keeps all of my dreams clearly in view at all times, tirelessly giving of himself to make them all come true and sharing all aspects of his life with me – my husband, my soul mate, my partner, my teacher, my confidant and my best friend, **Kevin Bailey**. "With every sunrise, I love you more."

ABOUT THE AUTHOR

Dr. James J. Mellon received his Doctorate in Consciousness Studies from Emerson Theological Institute and is an ordained Religious Science Minister with more than 20 years of service to his Spiritual Community. He spends his time between Los Angeles and Palm Desert, California, and is the Founding Spiritual Director of Global Truth Center Los Angeles, as well as Spiritual Director for the Spiritual Center of the Desert, both spiritual communities of love and unconditional acceptance. Combining the arts with spirituality is Dr. James' primary focus and his personal vision of "Enlightenment Through Entertainment" inspires his ministry.

Prior to becoming a minister, Dr. James had a successful career in the entertainment industry, including Broadway, television, music and film. He played Riff in the Jerome Robbins revival of "West Side Story" and toured the country as Jesus in "Jesus Christ Superstar" before turning his attention to directing and writing. He has written for television and film and has had three original musicals published for which he has written the book, music and lyrics. His first book, "Mental Muscle, 16-Weeks of Spiritual Boot Camp" has gone through three printings and is being used by many centers and workshops around the world. His prosperity program, "Core Prosperity Relief" (CPR) has attracted thousands of participants for each 30-day workshop. His program on physical health and well-being, "B.O.D.S. (Building Our Dynamic Selves)," uses quantum physics as a backdrop for how the body/mind connection can restore our bodies to their most vital expression. And his new book, "THE FIVE QUESTIONS," will be released at the end of 2022.

Dr. James and his husband, Broadway producer and actor Kevin Bailey, have been together more than 30 years. Their son William is a 2022 graduate of Texas State University and is an aspiring screenwriter/director. Their daughter Nora, Will's twin, made her transition in 2018 and continues providing the family with her love, light, and guidance.

For more on Dr. James, please check out his website: jamesmellon.org.

"My Global Intention is to empower people to know that they can have it all, not because of what they do, but because of who they are."
— Dr. James Mellon

www.ingramcontent.com/pod-product-compliance
Lightning Source LLC
Chambersburg PA
CBHW071425090426
42737CB00011B/1569